GW01057443

Dream Ticket®
Business Strategy
in the Digital Age

Annie Brooking

PublishNation
www.publishnation.co.uk

Table of Contents

This book is dedicated to entrepreneurs who decide to "have a go". Those who work 24/7 for years on end to achieve their dreams, and even when they fail, get up, dust themselves off and have another go.

Finally to Leighton for his unwavering support and love.

Acknowledgements

It's taken 30 years to gather the knowledge to write this book so I can't imagine how many people I need to thank for their help.

I'd like to thank Simon Portman at Marks&Clark, the patent agents and legal firm. Simon read drafts of this manuscript and gave really helpful feedback. Thanks to Philip Martin and Bella Schuckburgh also from Marks&Clark for their support and help to refine my ideas into Dream Ticket® Seminars.

I'd like to thank Billy Wang and Anna Mieczakowski who gave detailed feedback on my manuscript and Lucy Saunders, Shaun Househam and Toby Rickett who listened to audio versions of this book.

Finally to Lulu at Pitaya for her book cover design which I love.

Chapter 1

Why Business Planning is hard

Business planning and hitting business goals is hard, especially if you are a new company with no historical data to aid in the forecasting process.

Yet all businesses need to plan to grow and generate revenue to pay the bills and employees, raise investment capital and give good returns to shareholders. If you are bringing new products to market you will need to make strategic product marketing plans to ensure that when the product hits the market it's well accepted and gets traction quickly.

Over the years I have probably written over a hundred business and product-to-market plans and mentored over 60 CEOs to do the same thing. I have experienced bringing very successful products to market but also had some failures along the way.

When I look at the failures these were my most common mistakes

1. Predicting the time to market adoption
2. Generating timely brand recognition
3. Underestimating the time to comply with standards
4. Underestimating the time to change poor "Positioning"

5. Underestimating the time it would take for a product to get out of "The Void"
6. The importance of great investor relations
7. Not having sufficient product or endorsements and peer reviews
8. Underestimating the difficulty to motivate distributors to sell
9. The difficulty in attracting and retaining a great Board of Advisors
10. Having reliable manufacturing partners

Let's look at each one of these in a bit more detail.

1. Predicting the timing of market adoption

The product team has a tendency to fall in love with the product or service it's bringing to market. On one hand, the product team has to be passionate about the product and evangelize it when it's launched – yet they also need to be able to step back and look rationally at the product, warts and all. Why is it then that great products that deliver obvious benefits are not snapped up by the market? I wish I had a pound (or a dollar!) for every time someone has asked me "if this product really can pay for itself in a matter of months why isn't it selling?" The answer is simple. People don't like change, they like risk even less, it's safer to be part of a tribe.

2. Brand recognition

There is great security in being part of a tribe. If people you know and respect buy "Product X" then you will also feel safe to buy it. When I first heard the name "Airbnb" I asked if anyone in the office had heard of them. Everyone had, except me! After five minutes of hearing how great they were I booked accommodation. Brand recognition by trusted peers is a safety blanket. So the process of building brand recognition should be very high up on the list of every product marketer.

3. Compliance with standards

Some products have standards they must comply with. Standards help to indicate that a product is of a certain level of quality and almost instantly generate trust even in situations where a given brand is not yet well recognised.

Medical and food products have FDA to consider. Most countries have their own safety standards to comply with. In general, compliance with a given standard is an important validation and tick box activity. Sometimes there are no mandatory standards for a product to comply with, and sometimes there are no existing standards for a product to comply with at all. Yet if the customer *thinks* it should be complying with a standard it does not need, or worse cannot comply with, you have a bad Positioning problem. Until the standards box is ticked the customer won't buy. So you have to find a tick box that will satisfy the customer.

Where products or services do comply with standards such as FDA, various ISO standards or medical device directives this adds value to the company and is frequently the trigger for a customer to purchase. As such they are an asset.

4. Underestimating the time to change poor "Positioning"

Positioning happens in the mind of the prospect. Positioning is the one thing the prospect *thinks* when he hears the name of your product. Ideally, you want the prospect to think what you want him to think and that might be a tagline, or jingle. It must be a positive thought that makes him inclined to purchase. Examples include

For a real estate app - "Helps me sell my house faster"

For a burger chain "Great customer service",

For a laser printer "Fabulous value for money"

For a car "Keeps my family safe"

If the Positioning is off-message or worse negative "It's expensive", "It doesn't work", "It's difficult to use" the customer will not buy and it will take a long time to shift that position in his head. You may have to spend years repositioning or even rename, re-brand and re-launch.

5. Underestimating the time it would take for a product to get out of The Void

Famous marketer Geoffrey A Moore wrote the textbook for high tech marketers "Crossing the Chasm" which outlines the different categories of customers: technology enthusiasts, visionaries, early adopters, early majority and laggards pointing out that each of these categories have different product expectations and thus require different marketing strategies to encourage them to buy. In 2010 I identified an additional pre-chasm phase which I called "The Void".

Avoid the Void!

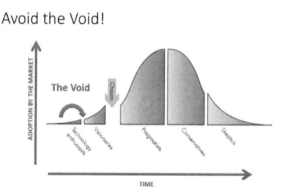

Figure 1 the Void

(*"The VOID and the Chasm: Planning and Developing Products that use Disruptive Technology", 17th International Product Development Conference", Murcia, Spain June 2010*).

The VOID occurs when you engage with the first adopter group and they respond to the product proposition with *"I don't believe it"*.

This is very bad news for marketers as prospects won't buy until they prove to themselves that the product really does do what is says on the can. Getting out of the Void involves free trials, demonstration units and endorsements from trusted individuals and organisations all of which takes a long time and lots of money.

6. The Importance of great investor relations

Having great investor relations is a key success factor for companies as they can bring much more than money to the table, including customers, potential distributors and also new investors. Whilst there may be no legal requirement for all companies to have regular shareholder meetings and investor updates it's wise to invest in this time as you never know when you may require their support. When joining a business as a CEO you may be inheriting a disillusioned investor base whose expectations may have been mismanaged by previous management or just poor market conditions.

7. Having sufficient endorsements and peer reviews

Mature products sometimes have hundreds of endorsements that make them much easier to sell. I recently read of a US salesman selling life insurance whose sole marketing material was a folder of over 100 customer letters, reviews and endorsements. He simply handed the folder over to his prospect. By page ten most had agreed to purchase.

New products may have no endorsements and of course nobody wants to be first to buy (except maybe "technology enthusiasts"). Getting endorsements may require giving products and services away or heavy discounting in return for endorsements and peer reviews. Again this takes a lot of time and is costly.

8. The difficulty in motivating distributors to sell a product

Recruiting distributors and managing them is a really valuable skill to have in the business. Bad distributor management results in low or no sales. New distributors are typically enthusiastic but still require a huge amount of support, training, motivation and constant "deals" to keep them selling.

Distributors will always go for low hanging fruit that delivers the greatest revenue, so if you don't make it easy for them to sell they won't bother. Once a distributor has gone off the boil it's unlikely they can be re-motivated.

9. The difficulty in attracting and retaining a great Board of Advisors

Having people to help open doors is extremely valuable. Having a great board is wonderful. Having a bad or demanding one can take over the life of a CEO. Being subjugated to a demanding majority shareholder just knocks the enthusiasm out of a management team, worse it can render them dysfunctional. Where a board is solely made up of investors there is no room for industry sector advisors who can introduce customers, help with strategies to enter new markets and provide a sounding board for the management team. This is when an Advisory Board is very helpful. Cash strung companies may have to incentivise advisors with options or stock, but it is worth keeping in mind that an Advisory Board will need to change over time as the needs of the company change.

10. Having reliable manufacturing partners

A quality manufacturing partner is a key asset for a company that sells tangible products. In the perfect scenario, the manufacturer is in such synergy with the company that goods can be shipped directly to the customer from the factory with no need for the company to get involved in testing, quality issues or shipping. This may take a while to achieve, maybe years.

Unreliable manufacturing partners who don't test products properly and cause products to be shipped that fail on arrival with the customer, should be replaced. This is a hard decision to make as these relationships take years to build yet are a key asset to the credibility of the company as in the customer's eyes the product just doesn't work. He does not care why or who is responsible.

Notice in the above paragraph I have referred to having a *great manufacturing partner* as a corporate asset – also *compliance with standards*. In fact, if you revisit the list above they are all situations and if each of these situations was in really great shape they would all be a valuable company assets.

Not one of these assets is tangible. They are all business assets that you can't touch or feel yet they have the power to bring a business to its knees and fail. They are intangible assets and as such form part of what is referred to as part of the *"Intellectual Capital"* of a business.

The interesting thing about my challenges in building successful businesses is that each challenge above describes a "situation" and many are related to time and getting timing right is key to hitting business goals

However as situations, they can be managed, changed and turned into positive outcomes.

No doubt each of you has your own war stories to tell. Thinking about some of your past experiences in bringing products to market that did not go as planned, I am guessing that they mostly included situations that did not pan out as you had predicted and so may have been things like:

- Customers wanted to try before they bought
- The sales cycle was longer than anticipated
- It took over a year to get brand recognition
- Getting customer endorsements took six months longer than we planned
- Customers did not believe the product could actually do what we said it could

If each of these situations were reversed so they were:

- Customers bought after just one demonstration
- We managed to build the brand in six months
- We had 20 customer endorsements on the web site in four months
- The product features perfectly matched customer expectations

Looking at the revised list of situations, these would have made it much easier to be successful. These situations are business assets. They are not hard assets, like trucks, buildings and so forth they are intangible assets and as such form part of what is called the Intellectual Capital of the business, which we will discuss next.

Finding Intellectual Capital

In the mid-1990s I was looking at high tech start-up companies and helping them create product-to market strategies and business plans to raise venture capital, I still do that today. Many of these companies only had intangible assets. Valuing businesses that only have intangible assets (intellectual property, brands, key founders, software and so forth) and have few tangible assets (buildings, factories, machinery, fleets of vehicles) turns out to be extremely difficult as their value is context dependent. To the right partner they are valuable yet to another they have no value.

So I set out to build a methodology to value intangible assets in monetary terms. Sadly I failed, as in each case the value was different to different investors or acquirers. The value was in the eye of the beholder. They are only worth what someone is prepared to pay for them unlike most tangible assets that have a recognised "book value".

Fortunately whilst on this journey, I discovered something far more powerful. If you had the right set of "assets" and they were very strong the company had a great chance of hitting its goals, of being successful. So I set about defining a list of intangible assets that would be relevant to most businesses. Different types of businesses have a different subset of intangible assets. I devised a method to look at these assets which I called an Intellectual Capital Audit which Identified and documented each asset and recorded it in an Intellectual Capital database.

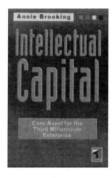 

Figure 1.2 Intellectual Capital and Corporate Memory

This exercise culminated in my writing the first book on Intellectual Capital which was published in 1999, shortly followed by a book on Knowledge Management called *Corporate Memory*.

What I did not realise at the time was that the measurement and management of intangible assets actually formed the basis for the business plan and much more.

Thus Dream Ticket® was born.

The Dream Ticket® is the set of strong intangible assets that a company would need to have if it was going to be successful, to have a home run.

So getting back to my original question "Why is it hard to write a business plan?"

The answer is it's hard to write a business plan because it requires the author to "*know*" what the business will look like three to five years from now.

In the absence of a crystal ball, it's hard to see into the future.

We don't plan tasks that deliver a conducive future environment where a product, service or business is able to thrive.

We have not been planning to grow intangible assets, because we don't know what they are supposed to look like in three years' time.

However now there is a way to solve this problem and that's what the rest of this book is about, but before we look at how to see into the future let's look at the different types of intangible assets and how they add value to a business.

Introducing Intangible Assets

Intangible assets are assets that typically don't take a physical form. In my book *"Intellectual Capital"* I split them into four categories: market assets, intellectual property assets, infrastructure assets and human centred assets. In the next four chapters, I have listed the most common 46 assets spread across the four categories. Every company is different so not all assets will be relevant to all companies. The largest category of assets is market assets and it's interesting to note that in 1999 I identified a list of around a dozen market assets. Today that number has doubled. This is primarily due to the advent of social media which has revolutionised the way businesses seek to attract and engage with their customers. In response to high technology product evolution, there are a couple of new categories of intellectual property assets and a couple of Infrastructure assets which relate to social media management systems. Human centred assets have not changed!

I have often been asked why I don't include tangible assets such as trucks or buildings in my method. The reason for this should become clearer when we go through the Dream Ticket® process but the purpose of identifying intangible is that they describe a "situation" which we are going to manipulate in the Dream Ticket® process and it's typically the case that tangible assets pan out as facilitators. Take the situation of a haulage company. Having a fleet of 500 trucks is certainly an asset but only if they are appropriately deployed, so the asset would be 1000 customers with repeat business that the trucks would facilitate.

Anyhow please feel free to use my process for business benefit – if it is useful for you to modify it, be my guest!

The 46 asset set is also available as a card deck called BIZVIZ® (short for Business Visualisation) from www.magicmonkey.eu . Business Visualisation is the process we are going to explore in the next few chapters.

Figure 1.3 the BIZVIZ® Card Deck

Chapter 1 Summary

1. Creating successful strategies and plans is difficult as you need to be able to predict what the company will need in the future
2. Business strategy and hitting goals is hard without historical data
3. Planning involves managing future "situations" that will be advantageous to the business
4. Many of today's companies only have intangible assets
5. A company's collection of intangible assets is called Intellectual Capital
6. Each company will have its unique set of intangible assets it needs to be successful
7. A Dream Ticket® is the set of strong intangible assets that a company needs to hit its goals
8. Having the "right" set of intangible assets that are in good shape means the company should be able to hit its goals

Chapter 2

Introducing Market Assets

In this chapter we will look at the first of the four categories of intangible assets, market assets. In my mind market assets are extremely important assets and typically the largest category for most companies. Without them it's impossible to do business.

Market assets are assets that give a company power in the marketplace. Businesses might have no intellectual property, few infrastructure assets and few human-centred assets, but if they don't have rich market assets, they will die. So it's not surprising that market assets are the largest category in the Business Visualisation Methodology.

Market assets include brands, names (company, product and/or service), positioning, taglines, jingles, tribes, on-line communities, repeat business, evangelists, endorsements and social media. When a company is under financial pressure, the first thing that management tends to cut is the development and management of market assets. This is like stopping a top athlete from going to the gym and training but still expecting them to win.

Market assets have never been more important than they are today as so many businesses, customers and colleagues fight for our attention. Market assets have doubled in number over the last 20 years due to the rise of social media and the fact that every business must have a web presence. Market assets also require new skills to grow and manage them.

MARKET ASSETS: Names

Naming is great fun. It's also a challenge as most of the best names have already been taken. Names have to be unforgettable, easy to spell and appropriate for your product or company. A premium product or service needs to have a name that reflects that.

When naming a company, take care to consider the risks involved in having a functional name, one that describes what the company does. The company might change its product or service offering as it evolves. I made this mistake when I founded The Technology Broker as a technology licensing company, because it finished up offering mentoring services to start-up CEOs raising venture capital.

Engineers love to name products with technical terms, differentiating products with numbers 'AllTest-1204', 'AllTest-1743' – no one will remember these names. Even more forgettable are names that are a union of the owners, B&K Building, APB Plumbing Services.

A great source of help when choosing names is www.igorinternational.com, who have a lot of advice and information on their website.

Q1. Does your company have a great and memorable name?

Q2. Are your product names easy to spell?

Q3. Is the domain available?

MARKET ASSETS: Brands

A good brand will differentiate you from your competitors and give your product a certain market position if supported with appropriate promotion. The trick is to find a great name for a brand, and naming is very hard. Ideally, brands also have to be unique so that a domain name can be registered, and now getting a unique domain name is a challenge. The brand name may be the same as the company name if there is only one product but, obviously, if you have more than one product a different brand name for each, whether or not used in conjunction with the company name, is preferable.

When designing a brand, it's also important to consider how to protect it with a trademark. The key thing to avoid is being 'descriptive', as that would prevent a brand being protected by a trademark. Most countries have a trademark registry which you can search on-line to see if your brand has been marked by anyone already.

In designing a brand, it is best to make up a word – like NESPRESSO®, which is a clever combination of Nestle® and espresso.

Q1. Do you have branded products?

Q2. Are your brands memorable?

Q3. Does your target customer remember your brand?

MARKET ASSETS: Positioning

Positioning happens in the mind of the listener when they hear your product or company name. Positioning and position are not the same. You will hear marketers talk about how their product is positioned in the market against the competition. This refers to USPs (unique selling propositions) which are determined as part of competitive analysis, but it's not positioning. Great positioning is a huge asset.

Positioning is typically captured in a short statement - the Positioning Statement. Ideally you want your prospect to hear and think what you want them to hear and think. Promotional campaigns support a product's positioning in the market place. Avis the car rental firm kicked off a TV positioning campaign in 1978 which used the tag line 'We try harder', posing the question in the prospect's mind, 'harder than who?' At the time, the market leader was Hertz, so the positioning was 'Avis tries harder than Hertz'. Great stuff, this is exactly the message Avis wanted their prospects and customers to think, and they did.

Q1. What is your Positioning Statement?

Q2. What do want your prospects to think when they hear your company/product name?

Q3. What do they think now? Ask them.

MARKET ASSETS: Brand Recognition

Having a great brand is all well and good, but not if no-one recognises it. The first step in making a sale is to get your product in front of the customer and get them to remember the brand name.

There is also a tribal thing that goes on with brand recognition. If two of your prospects meet and one asks the other about your product and gets a positive response, 'Oh yes, I've heard about X', it gives the questioner a type of security. If a large percentage of your target audience recognises your brand and it is positioned positively, you should begin to see brand recognition.

Consider a very novel PhD invention for identifying skin cancer called SIAscopy. When the product came to market branded the SIAscope, the target audience had heard of it, but it was positioned in their minds as 'an interesting little research project'. So guess what? They did not purchase. When the SIAscope was rebranded as MoleMate®, it began to sell.

Q1. What percentage of your prospects recognise your brand?

Q2. Does your brand reflect your positioning?

Q3. Is your brand working for you or against you?

MARKET ASSETS: Tag Lines

Tag lines and positioning go hand in hand. A great tag line can generate decades of market value. It's a short snappy line which is memorable.

My absolute favourite is 'Should've gone to SpecSavers'®, which is the tag line of a company that sells spectacles via a franchise model. It's also a trademark. The tag line has been promoted successfully via a very funny TV ad campaign that shows people making blunders because they're not wearing spectacles, the tag line popping up at the end of the ad. This particular tag line has migrated its way into daily use, with people saying 'Should've gone to Specsavers' when they have made a mistake. Pure gold.

Some tag lines are so successful that, after a while, a single word or image in an ad prompts the viewer to finish the tag line in their head. The Australian actor Paul Hogan of *Crocodile Dundee* fame started his career advertising Winfield cigarettes in Australia. The tag line 'Anyhow have a Winfield' morphed over time into a fast shot of Hogan just saying 'Anyhow'.

Q1. Does your company have a tag line?

Q2. Should your products/services have tag lines?

Q3. Where would you promote them?

MARKET ASSETS: Jingles

A jingle is a musical tag line. Probably the most successful and long standing is that for 'Intel Inside'. It started in 1970 as a tag line, 'The Computer Inside', which was voiced. Over the years, it morphed into 'Intel Inside', also voiced. In 1994, the now famous jingle 'the Intel Bong', five perfect notes, was added and the voice-over was dropped. It's said to be worth millions of dollars.

Another oldie is the Green Giant 'HoHoHo Green Giant', which was introduced in 1958, now that's longevity!

A key component is that the product name sticks in your head. If the tune is irritatingly catchy so the audience sings along, great. If it stays in their head, it's a winner.

Musical jingles with no vocals have another great advantage, they are international and don't have to be translated, so they have the potential for global recognition. Also bear in mind that jingles can be trademarked in the same way words and logos can.

Of course not everyone can afford TV advertising, but it's not expensive to make your own videos and incorporate them into your web site making it stickier.

Q1. Could your company use a jingle?

Q2. Where would you promote it?

Q3. Can your Positioning Statement be a jingle?

MARKET ASSETS: Suspects, Prospects, Customers and Evangelists

Thinking about the sales pipeline, how do you categorise the companies in it? I use four categories.

Firstly Suspects. These are companies or people you suspect could buy your product or service. For example, if you are selling life insurance, you might target fathers aged 25-35. However, they might already have a policy, be out of work, or not be able to afford the payments. So until you qualify them, they are a suspect. Once qualified, they become a prospect and then go into the sales pipeline. If the prospect purchases, they become a customer.

When there is no clear differentiation between suspects and prospects, the sales forecast will be misleading. This is when sales targets get missed.

However, the most valuable asset is the customer who is so happy with the experience they have had with your company that they become an evangelist and talk or write about your company in glowing terms. They are precious.

Q1. Do you have a clear, agreed distinction between suspects and prospects?

Q2. Think about your customer base, can you identify ten Evangelists?

Q3 Will they collaborate with you in promotional activities?

MARKET ASSETS: Tribes

Master marketer Seth Godin wrote the definitive text on tribes. He defines a tribe as 'A group of people connected to one another, connected to a leader, connected to an idea'.

There are many tribes in the computer industry, called user groups. Some of them are very powerful and large, notably Apple's user group, which has hundreds of branches globally representing every walk of life. Together, they are an Apple tribe.

As a tribe, they are a great resource for Apple. Not only can Apple upsell more product to them, but tribe members also willingly test new products and act as Apple evangelists.

It is helpful to know if your prospects are organised as a tribe, for instance in a professional organisation, or as a group of people who do the same job in different geographies. If your prospect base is not organised as a tribe, it will be harder to promote and market as they are difficult to get to. On-line communities may or may not be a tribe.

Q1. Do your customers and prospects belong to a tribe?

Q2. Do you have a way to influence or lead this tribe?

Q3. Should you be starting a tribe?

MARKET ASSETS: Endorsements

Endorsements are when a customer or colleague writes or speaks positively about you or your company. An example is LinkedIn endorsements, which tend to be tit-for-tat, I endorse you if you endorse me – so not quite as powerful as we might like.

Far better is to film your customers talking about your products or services. A brilliant example comes from digital media gurus Exposure Ninja. The video is bang in the middle of the home page on their web site and introduced by head ninja Tim Kitchen. The four-minute video comprises nine customer endorsements spliced with eight of Tim's ninjas talking enthusiastically about their company and their work. That's a lot of valuable content in four minutes that's not necessarily expensive to produce. If you are nervous about doing it yourself, there are lots of companies around that will do a pretty good two to four-minute video for a very reasonable price

Q1. Do you have any video endorsements on your website?

Q2. Are they right up front on the home page or hidden in a menu?

Q3. Do you have six evangelists who would be in your video?

MARKET ASSETS: Repeat Business

If you have customers that keep coming back for more product, they are an asset. If they are locked-in in some way, even better. That's why investors love products with consumables that represent repeat business – the razor/razorblade model.

If pull for the consumable becomes significant, you can expect a predator to get in on the act and copy the consumable. Legal agreements in your Infrastructure Assets can help by informing the customer that the product is not warranted or will be not be serviced if consumables are not purchased from your company.

That said, you can't take repeat business for granted, so these customers should be at the top of your care list to make sure they don't jump ship. We all know it takes a lot of work and money to find a new customer, so repeat business is the most cost-effective option for sales.

Q1. Who are your repeat customers?

Q2. When was the last time they had a courtesy call from someone senior in the company?

Q3. Is there some way you could introduce a repeat business offering into your product line?

MARKET ASSETS: Backlog

Backlog are orders that have come in but are not yet fulfilled. These are an asset as they are future revenue.

Sometimes it's possible to get orders based on hitting key performance indicators to a timetable. This is common with new products where the customer wants evidence that the product works and asks for a free trial. These relationships need very careful babysitting to ensure the trial is conducted to plan.

The worst case of backlog management I have seen was when a California laptop manufacturer needed a flat rectangular battery for a new laptop design. An entrepreneur proposed a specification and got a PO for $1 million. With this he raised $1 million in venture capital. Months later he showed up at the laptop company with the working battery. They were surprised, as they had not heard from him for months and in the meantime had changed the footprint of the laptop. The battery did not fit. The entrepreneur lost the deal and the VC $1 million.

Q1. Does your company regularly have backlog?

Q2. Is there any way you can build a backlog?

Q3. Do you take great care with backlog relationships?

MARKET ASSETS: Web Sites

A web site is a corporate asset, but only if it is very well designed and regularly maintained. The web site is the heart of the digital marketing strategy. You can pay exactly the same to get a bad web site as you can to get a great one.

The key is to make the web site generate business for you, and that probably means getting a copywriter to rewrite your content so it sells.

To be a great asset, your web site needs to be fresh, have calls to action on every page, have your contact number on every page and have short punchy videos to sell your products, services and company. Include testimonials, and make sure search engine optimisation, SEO, is built into the web site from day one. Some companies, such as www.exposureninja.com, will do a free web site review.

Q1. What free calls to action can I offer on my web site?

Q2. How sticky is my web site. What great advice and tips can I offer prospects to visit and stay on it?

Q3. Could my web site benefit from copywriting services?

MARKET ASSETS: High Click Through, Low Bounce

Click-through rate (CTR) is the ratio of users who *click* on a specific link to the number of total users who view a page, email, or advertisement. It is commonly used to measure the success of an online advertising campaign for a particular website as well as the effectiveness of email campaigns.

A high CTR is a good indication that users find your ads useful and relevant, meaning you're probably touching your target audience.

A low bounce rate is an indicator of a sticky web site and this is what the web site should be designed to deliver. If your web site has a high bounce rate, it means someone is landing on one of your pages and then leaving. This could be for several reasons. If your web site is slow loading, old or not easy to navigate, people will bounce off. If someone lands on a page other than your home page, make sure there are internal links so they do not bounce.

Q1. Do you know what your CTR and bounce rates are?

Q2. Is your primary message repeated on most pages?

Q3. Are you using social media dashboards?

MARKET ASSETS: Digital Media Strategy

The digital media strategy will be different depending on what type of company you have, B2B or B2C. The age and gender of the target audience is also a factor in the platforms you choose to promote the business. To explore the demographics of the major social media platforms, look at www.sproutsocial.com.

There are many different platforms available, and new ones pop up all the time. The key is to understand the demographics of each platform and choose the most appropriate mix, so that they work together to drive prospects to your web site for help, advice and information about your products and services. It's better to have a small amount of quality content than pushing out content daily for the sake of keeping your name in the media. If your posts and blogs are not useful to your target audience, they will get into the habit of deleting them on sight. If you don't have in-house digital media experts, outsource and work closely with your chosen providers.

Q1. Do we have a digital media strategy?

Q2. Who manages it? Is it effective in driving sales?

Q3. Should you outsource?

MARKET ASSETS: Hashtags

Designated by a #, the hashtag is paired with a word or phrase making it searchable. Creating a notable hashtag as part of the social media strategy can be a business asset.

Unfortunately you cannot own a hashtag. You can trade mark a hashtag, but that won't stop people from using it, so the trick is to create a unique hashtag that's easy to remember and can be associated with your company, branding, products and services. It is possible to have a design right on a hashtag.

If you are running workshops or seminars, you can use a hashtag in advance of the event to help promote it by including it on all promotional media.

Hashtags need to be unique, as sometimes the same hashtag is used for different purposes. It's best to do a hashtag search before promoting a new hashtag, so your community does not get confused.

Q1. What hashtags are associated with your company, brands and products?

Q2. What is your policy for 'managing' who is tweeting with these hashtags?

Q3. Are you including your high-profile hashtags in all of your marketing material?

MARKET ASSETS: Online Communities

An online community is a group of people that could be interested in your products or services. If your business has a principal who is the leader of that community, so much the better. On-line communities can also be tribes such as Linked-In Groups, which typically focus on a particular market sector, for instance waste water management, bakery or even frozen chicken feet. By joining a group and participating in conversations, you connect with people who are like-minded.

Different social media platforms offer different types of communities. Those suitable for B2C might not work as well for B2B, it depends on what you want to sell or share.

When communicating with on-line communities, make sure the content is relevant to the group and positions your business as a thought-leader. If you are selling air conditioning equipment, don't post a picture of a giraffe with a funny neck! Best to communicate top quality content or not at all.

Q1. What on-line communities are relevant to your business?

Q2. Are you a member or leader of one?

Q3. Is the material you are posting or tweeting positioning your business appropriately?

MARKET ASSETS: Blogs

Blogging is a great way to establish yourself as a thought-leader and bring people to your web site. Find a topic where you have expertise that is valuable and relevant to your followers. If you are a company selling scientific consultancy, don't blog about 'How to interview employees'. A major issue for blogging success is how frequently you blog. I put this question to social media guru Tim Kitchen and his advice was to spend the time to write something excellent rather than dashing off something every other day. Tim says his most popular blogs are the ones he spends an entire weekend writing.

Conversely marketing guru Seth Godin blogs almost every day and is ranked number 1 in the top 50 Business Blogs. His blogs are much shorter, typically around 200 words, and cover a wide range of topics.

Running blogger events so other bloggers write about your business is an alternative, and unsurprisingly Tim Kitchen has a blog on how to do that too!

> **Q1. Who in your company blogs?**

> **Q2. Can you commit to create regular informative blogs?**

> **Q3. Do your blogs generate traffic to your web site and increase revenue?**

MARKET ASSETS: Videos

Videos are a great way to promote your company and introduce its services. Even better, videos that show your customers giving testimonials are a great business asset, especially if they are slap bang in the middle of your home page. Not only should videos be on your web site as they will make it stickier, but also on YouTube. There are several companies that will make short videos for your business at very reasonable rates.

Product videos are also a great way of explaining how your products work, and can also show that they are simple, and easy to operate, maintain, service and more.

Showing your team in a video adds a lovely personal touch to a website. They can be talking about the product and the company, its values and what it's like to work there.

Q1. Should you have videos on your web site?

Q2. Are your products hard to explain over the phone? If they are, a video might be helpful.

Q3. Should you make a video showing your employees talking about the company or its products and services?

MARKET ASSETS: The Distribution Channel

Companies that choose to sell products indirectly have to put a huge amount of work into developing a really good distribution channel, and there are certain people who excel at doing this.

By definition, the distribution channel is frequently not local (or you'd be doing it yourself), so figuring out exactly what your distributor is doing (or not doing) with your product can be hard, especially if you don't have the funds to hop onto a plane regularly and meet them face to face. New distributors are mostly keen when they sign up but their enthusiasm wanes if the product or service is difficult or expensive to sell.

Using agents is an alternative (they get a commission when their leads turn into customers who buy), but having them focus on your product when they represent several others as well is a challenge.

Basically, the distribution channel will focus on what's easiest to sell that will earn them the most money with least effort, so managing them is a 24/7 job.

Q1. Is indirect sales the right channel for your company?

Q2. How frequently do you audit the channel?

Q3. What would your channel members say about your company?

MARKET ASSETS: Franchisees

Franchising is an alternative business model where you have a 'recipe' for a business that you franchise to other companies so they can emulate it. Famous franchise businesses include MacDonald's, Pizza Hut, KFC, 7-Eleven, educational programme Nutty Scientists, and dry cleaners Prima Master.

If you have a business idea that can be turned into a 'recipe', then franchise could be an option for a market asset. However, there is a lot of work to do setting up a franchise model, as you have to develop a manual that tells the franchisee exactly what to do from day 1, and also includes a training programme. Franchising is also subject to various regulations so you should seek legal advice when setting one up. Franchise law is a special type of contract law as the customer needs to get exactly the same product or service from a franchisee in the USA or India (well nearly!).

Q1. Is there any part of your business that is appropriate for franchise?

Q2. Could your product or service be homogeneous in different geographies?

Q3. Could you write a manual to explain exactly how your business does what it does?

Chapter 2 Summary

1. Market assets give a company power in the marketplace
2. Market assets are more important today due to the advent of digital media
3. Product names must be easy to spell and not functional
4. Choose brands that can be trademarks
5. Positioning is the most powerful marketing tool in your toolkit
6. Regularly survey for brand recognition
7. Have one great tag line
8. Have clear definitions for suspects and prospects
9. Can you own and lead a tribe?
10. Strive for endorsements and evangelists
11. Make sure your web site is bringing you business, get it audited
12. Consider outsourcing your digital media strategy
13. If you blog make them really good
14. Put a customer endorsement video bang in the middle of your home page
15. Regularly audit the distribution channel

Chapter 3

Introducing Intellectual Property (IP) Assets

Intellectual property (IP) assets are assets of the mind that are protectable in law, and typically go hand in hand with Market and Infrastructure Assets.

IP assets are probably the best known intangible asset and consist of patents, trademarks, copyright, trade secrets, design rights and some special IP categories (for instance semi-conductor topography rights and database rights).

Patents help protect products and services. The first US patent was issued in 1790, and over 6 million more have been issued since then in the US alone.

Trademarks protect brands and hashtags, and copyright protects software, databases, web sites, designs and music. In turn, licence agreements provide the legal infrastructure to generate revenue from copyright. Non-disclosure agreements protect trade secrets. Design rights protect the look and feel, or design, of a product.

The value of an IP portfolio is peculiar to the potential acquirer and the value of many high technology companies is locked into their IP portfolio. This is particularly true of genomics, pharmaceutical and semiconductor companies.

IP Assets: Patents

A patent is a property right which is granted by the State to the inventor to protect an invention. It's a monopoly right and, if granted, typically has a life of 20 years. The right is exclusive in a territory or country. Patents are extremely important intangible assets for several reasons, most notably:

1. They protect a product and give the inventor a monopoly right.
2. They act as a 'KEEP OFF' sign for competitors.

Not all inventions can be patent protected as they have to comply with requirements for novelty, inventive step, and industrial application, and not include excluded material (they can't be immoral, for example).

There is no such thing as a global patent, so the key issue is, 'Will it give me a business advantage in the territory it is protected in?' Fees for maintaining a patent for 20 years can grow to be massive, so calculating the ROI is important and having a patent agent who is business savvy is a must. The patent portfolio should be audited annually.

Q1. Should/could your company have a patent portfolio?

Q2. Can you detail the business proposition for each patent?

Q3. Could you generate revenue from licensing?

IP Assets: Copyright

Copyright is a proprietary right which protects original literary, artistic, musical, sound, film, and broadcast work. This also includes websites, apps, and software, although some software can also be patented. To be covered by copyright, the work must be original. Unlike patents, copyright does not have to be 'registered', the mere fact that it is authored and original is enough, although in some countries it is possible to register a work for copyright.

Copyright lasts for the lifetime of the author plus 70 years. There are some misconceptions about copyright ownership, the most frequent being that if you pay someone to write something or design your website, the copyright automatically resides with you because you paid for it. This is not the case, as copyright resides with the author unless assigned otherwise. This creates the possibility of the contractor suing you for copyright infringement of their work! To avoid this, make sure that the copyright or title in subcontracted work is assigned to you. It's wise to add the © symbol where appropriate.

Q1. What business critical works are copyright?

Q2. Do you have assignments for subcontracted work?

Q3. Are your employees aware of the rules of copyright?

IP Assets: Trade Secrets

When you file a patent, it is ultimately put into the public domain. This means that a competitor could use it – patent infringement is not illegal, the owner has to sue. So sometimes it's better to keep the secret private within the company.

If it becomes necessary to share the secret, the other party should sign a Confidentiality or Non-Disclosure Agreement (NDA). This is a contract between parties who agree to keep the secret. An NDA typically states that the secret is not in the public domain and when it is the recipient is off the hook. NDAs are typically for a fixed number of years, say three.

Putting 'CONFIDENTIAL' on a document before sending it to someone or telling them it is sensitive will flag up that they should keep it in confidence but it is far better to impose concrete and express obligations by getting them to sign an NDA.

When an employee signs an NDA on behalf of the company, he or she is binding the company, so it's important to make sure that employees working on the same project are aware of relevant signed NDAs.

Q1. What trade secrets do you have?

Q2. Who signs NDAs?

Q3. Are employees aware of the terms of signed NDAs?

IP Assets: Trademarks

A trademark is a registered mark which is associated with a company and its products. Trademarks typically protect logos, brands, hashtags and service brands (service marks). Trademarks guarantee the origin of goods and services and are designed to prevent 'passing off', which is where another company uses your mark or one very similar to it to confuse customers so they buy their products instead of yours.

A trademark is an asset as it can generate revenue, because it can be bought, sold or licensed. Trademarks can be national or within the EU as a Community Mark. Trademarks cannot be descriptive in language terms, which is why it's best to get creative as with the Nespresso® trade mark.

There are also on-line directories which can be searched. It's best to mark brands with a TM if they have not yet been registered. Once registered they should be accompanied with a 'Registered' symbol, ®.

Q1. Are you marking your products and services sufficiently with marks?

Q2. Are marks properly identified on all marketing material?

Q3. Are marks registered in important business territories?

IP Assets: Design Rights

Designs with 'eye appeal' can be registered with the Patent Office as a registered design. In the USA this is called a 'design patent'.

A design right typically protects the unique look of a product – the appearance and the combination of its shape, contours, colours etc. – so that consumers know that they are buying something authentic. Think of the shape of the first Crocs® on the market. In the UK you can protect a design for up to 25 years.

As with copyright, the design right stays with the designer, so if it was designed by a subcontractor the design right has to be assigned to be owned by the company. Design rights can be bought, sold or licensed for revenue.

There are also unregistered designs, which arise naturally and give the owner exclusive rights of reproduction, but the owner has to take steps to record the design in a document, sometimes mailing these to another party to prove the date of ownership.

Q1. Do you have products with unique eye appeal?

Q2. Have subcontracted designs for products been assigned to your company?

Q3. Is there any revenue that could be derived from licensing design rights?

IP Assets: Special IP Categories

Recently, new categories of IP have been developed to protect new kinds of products relating to our digital world.

The Semiconductor Topography Right was introduced to protect semiconductor products as neither patent nor copyright protection were sufficient for the industry. It's essentially a modified design right that is peculiar to the needs of the semiconductor industry. As the development time and cost of such products can be significant, the industry needed some form of legal protection for its investment, and the Semiconductor Topography Right came into force in 1986.

Another special IP category is the Database Right, which gives a company rights over the content of a database that it has created, so that its contents cannot be copied where there has been 'substantial investment' in obtaining, verifying or presenting the contents of the database. The term of the right is 15 years. Database Rights do not need to be registered. Genome databases are a good example of Database Rights.

Q1. Has your company invested substantial time and money in developing a proprietary database?

Q2. Could you build value into the company by creating a Database Right?

Q3. Who can identify whether you have a Database Right?

Chapter 3 Summary

1. IP assets are assets of the mind protectable in law
2. Trademarks can protect brands and hashtags
3. Copyright protects software, designs, databases, web sites and music
4. Licensing means copyright can be shared with more than one party for revenue
5. Just because you paid for copyright does not mean you own it, ownership must be assigned
6. Make sure patents are useful business assets and generate ROI
7. The life of a patent is typically 20 years
8. Protect valuable knowledge with trade secrets and non-disclosure agreements
9. Trademarks require registration, copyright does not
10. Products with "eye appeal" can be protected with a design right

Chapter 4

Introducing Infrastructure Assets

Infrastructure assets are important as they give a company internal strength. They are systems of all types: IT, standards, and shared beliefs. They are the skeleton of the business.

New companies won't have any infrastructure assets as they are built over time and require certain types of people to introduce and implement them. Established companies need to review infrastructure assets regularly as the world we work in is changing faster than ever before and it's important to ensure that infrastructure assets remain fit for purpose over time.

Infrastructure assets go hand in hand with IP assets by way of IP audits. Various legal agreements are required to enable revenue to be generated from franchising, licensing copyright and setting out how the distribution channel will work.

Some infrastructure assets are very intangible, such as corporate culture and management philosophy. These can be extremely difficult to change, so can be either a huge asset or, if not fit for purpose, a liability.

Infrastructure Assets: Corporate Culture

Corporate culture can best be described as 'The way we do things around here', and comprises values, heroes, rites and rituals, and group behaviours that are recognised and shared by all employees.

Corporate culture should keep the company safe from reacting to every market or management whim and mostly comes from the leadership of the company.

Virtual companies are becoming more prevalent as CEOs are discovering that it's more productive and profitable to be virtual, with employees all over the world working from home. Gone are the days when a 9-5 desk job or shift work were the only options.

Corporate cultures must support business goals and management style. Start-ups need a 'can do' culture as employees need to pitch in and do what's needed rather than waiting for instructions or sticking to their job specifications.

There are several different ways to categorise Corporate Culture: Control/Create/Collaborate/Compete, Family/Hero/Hierarchy, or Male/Female, etc. There is plenty of literature of the subject.

Q1. How would you describe your corporate culture?

Q2. Is it a business asset or liability?

Q3. Could culture change benefit the business?

Infrastructure Assets: Knowledge Management

It's worth considering just how much of a knowledge-based organisation your company is, where that knowledge resides, how valuable it is, how secure it is, and whether or not it should be more widely disseminated.

This is both a systems' issue and a human resource issue. Everyone is replaceable, but at what cost and over what period of time? Some competencies are easily replaced, others not so, especially when the competency is knowledge-based and that knowledge is tacit.

Thus identifying critical knowledge functions is a first step in knowledge management, together with identifying an individual in the company who can become the Knowledge Officer.

Documenting knowledge functions relating to the individual is a knowledge management process that should include education, hobbies, project experience, core competencies, mentors, mentees, publications, psychometric profile and the goals of each individual.

Building expert systems that embody critical knowledge functions is also an option, and this can be outsourced.

Q1. Do you know what your company knows?

Q2. What are your critical knowledge functions?

Q3. What knowledge management processes can you implement this month?

Infrastructure Assets: Management Philosophy

Management philosophy is the way company leaders think about their company and its employees. It encompasses guidance, direction, leadership and example setting, with the goal of bringing out the best in each employee and rewarding them accordingly.

The management philosophy of a company has a strong influence on corporate culture. Interestingly, in large organisations the perceived culture of top management can be very different to middle management and this can be detrimental to the business, especially where middle management are more concerned with keeping their jobs rather than doing what's best for the company.

Management philosophy should include encouraging feedback from employees so the process is kept fresh. Changes in the market may require new approaches, ideas and ways to motivate the team. That said, changing management philosophy and also corporate culture is very time consuming and costly. Sometimes, the only way to effect change is by removing the entire top layer of the company or ripping out middle management which, in both cases can create a knowledge management crisis.

Q1. What is the management philosophy in your company?

Q2. Are employees empowered?

Q3. Is management philosophy an asset or a liability?

Infrastructure Assets: Standards

Complying with various standards is important for a variety of reasons. Some standards are an essential pre-requisite to sales in certain territories, such as FDA approval for medical devices in the USA or ISO 13485 in the UK for medical device manufacturing. For some customers, quality standards are also a mandatory pre-requisite to purchase. These standards are valuable as they enable the marketability of products and services.

Standards are also a 'check box' for some customers, who feel more secure about a purchase if the company has its products 'approved'. This can happen even when approval is not required and there is no true need to adhere to a standard. Frustrating as it may be, the customer may not believe that to be the case, and will not purchase for that reason. Unfortunately, once the customer has it "positioned" in his head that the product is unapproved there is no way out of this conundrum.

Q1. Make a list of the standards your company complies with.

Q2. Do you promote compliance with these standards on all of your company's collateral?

Q3. What other standards would be of benefit to your company?

Infrastructure Assets: IT Systems

IT systems are essential infrastructure assets and new applications that may add value to the business in a variety of ways arrive on the market every day. They may be web based or internal, custom made or licensed products. Applications include CRM, project management, help desk, human resources, email marketing, billing and invoicing, and education. One thing is for sure – there are so many different applications on the market that there are bound to be some that your business does not have that could be of benefit.

New distributed database applications based on blockchain offer greater security and "trust" over conventional databases. However at the time of writing blockchain applications are not yet common other than for cryptocurrencies. A methodology to determine the nature of applications that should employ blockchain has not yet been developed.

You are probably thinking that finding out what you could use is a mammoth job. Not so. There are trusted organisations that will help you find applications and review them as well, for example the US company Software Advice.

Q1. What apps does your company use?

Q2. For a week, ask every business person you meet what apps they use. Make a list

Q3. Which functions in your company could be streamlined with an app?

Infrastructure Assets: The Board

The Board, including the Managing Director or CEO, should be an infrastructure asset. The Board should provide the business with services that ensure it complies with the legal and fiduciary requirements of the territory in which it is registered. The roles and responsibilities of directors is to assure the company's prosperity while meeting the appropriate interests of its shareholders.

The Board should provide the management with advice on the strategic direction of the company in response to their proposals, and assist in fundraising tactics and strategies. Boards vary in size and nature depending on the size and age of the company.

A key requirement of a non-executive Board member is that they understand the nature of the business and what the business needs in order to be successful. This might seem like stating the obvious, but if the Board has numerous investors as non-execs it may not leave enough seats for members from industry who could help the management team attract and retain business and contracts.

Q1. Is your company's Board an asset?

Q2. Is the Board visible to the company – in what way?

Q3. Does the Board help the business to attract business and contracts?

Infrastructure Assets: Shareholder and Investor Relations

The relationship that a company has with its shareholders and investors is a really important asset and it is worth putting special effort into shareholder and investor relations.

For public companies, there are mandatory procedures that must be followed.

For private companies, things are different. There is no requirement for private companies to have shareholder meetings or even communicate regularly with their investor base, but it is wise to aim for excellent investor relations, as you never know when you may need their help. A hundred people on your side can be quite an asset for attracting new business, investment and employees.

Crowdfunding has changed the investor landscape a lot as people who invest via crowdfunding platforms may be sophisticated investors or people having a punt for fun. The amount an investor puts in could be as little as a couple of hundred pounds or as much as several million, and a tiny company could end up with over a hundred shareholders to manage.

Q1. Does your company have a contented shareholder base?

Q2. How could shareholders help the company?

Q3. If you required more investment, would your investors all follow through?

Infrastructure Assets: Business and Management Processes

Business processes are designed to meet corporate goals and often have IT systems to support them. Most, if not all, businesses have internal procedures that they ought to use, but which sometimes fall by the wayside as other duties take priority.

The primary issue is whether or not business processes assist or inhibit business growth. A good business process (like Dream Ticket®!) should help the team to make good business decisions.

Another example is a market requirements document (MRD), which should be prepared before deciding whether to invest in a new product or service. The MRD covers more than 70 issues that should be considered before investment. The great thing about this process is that it forces the author(s) to examine a wide range of issues, including the market, customers, cost, competition, maintenance, manufacturing, and legal protection. The MRD works because it's very hard to contradict yourself and write nonsense when it's in black and white in front of you – but very easy to do if it's all in your head!

> **Q1. What business processes does your company have? Do they work?**
>
> **Q2. Are they appropriate and fit for purpose?**
>
> **Q3. How are they reviewed?**

Infrastructure Assets: Patent Audit Procedures

Having a patent portfolio should be an asset, but only if the patents have business relevance. Patents are expensive to maintain, especially if they are filed in numerous territories. Times change as does the market, so it's important to ensure that the business is getting good ROI on its patent portfolio.

Working with your patent attorney, you should design an audit procedure that you run through each year to help you decide whether or not a patent should be maintained or dropped in each territory. Key factors will be:

- whether the patent is protecting a product in a territory that delivers significant revenue
- whether the patent supports your competitive position
- whether it's a weak patent and funds could be better spent somewhere else.

There are two types of patent attorneys, those who will follow instructions and patent any invention regardless of its commercial relevance, and those who will challenge your request to file. The latter is preferable.

Q1. Do you regularly audit your patent portfolio?

Q2. Is your patent attorney commercially minded?

Q3. What is the business benefit of each patent in your portfolio?

Infrastructure Assets: Distribution Agreements

A distribution agreement is an asset that protects the company and sets out the conditions under which a third party may distribute your products and services. It typically includes targets for sales, the territory, confidentiality and the conditions under which the distributor may use your IP. It will also outline the duties of the distributor and your duties to them.

Almost everybody asks for an exclusive distribution agreement in a territory. This is a chicken and egg situation as you can't evaluate their performance until they have sold your products, and they can't commit to a sales target until they have proved to themselves that there is a market for your products in their territory. A new distributor's typical argument is that they will have to invest a lot of money in marketing before they know if they can be successful, so they request exclusive rights.

There is another consideration. Unless you have the bandwidth and experienced staff to train, support and manage the distribution channel, it will probably underperform.

Q1. Does your company have distributors?

Q2. Is there an annual review with the distributors?

Q3. How could you better support your distributors so they deliver more revenue?

Infrastructure Assets: Licence Agreements

A licence agreement is an agreement your company makes that allows another party to use your intellectual property in their own product or service. In return for the licence, the licensee pays a royalty. Huge revenues can be generated from licensing the right to merchandise products such as toys, t-shirts and games associated with hit movies. Just about anything that is covered by copyright can be licensed.

Software is copyright so although the physical media can be sold, the intellectual property in the code won't be sold to the customer, only licensed. Unlike a tangible asset, such as a pair of shoes (which can only be sold once), the same piece of software can be licensed (not sold) many times.

If your business plans to generate revenue from licensing, you need to have systems in place to track royalty payments as these are very frequently underpaid. This may not be because the licensee is being malicious, but because tracking is poor, or there are misunderstandings over when a royalty is due, for example in demonstration software or product trials.

Q1. Does your company license any of its intellectual property?

Q2. What royalty tracking systems do you have?

Q3. What intangible assets does your company have that could be licensed?

Infrastructure Assets: Franchise Agreements

A franchise agreement is a legally binding agreement which outlines the franchisor's terms and conditions for the franchisee. It also outlines the obligations of the franchisor and the obligations of the franchisee.

A franchise agreement is a special type of license where the franchisee's business is associated with the franchisor's brand and the franchisor provides significant assistance in how they use the brand in conducting their business. In return, the franchisee pays fees to the franchisor. These can include an initial fee and ongoing fees or percentages of profits.

Franchising involves a special kind of law that has its own experts, and they attempt to balance the need of the franchisor to protect their intellectual property and the needs of the franchisee to manage their independently owned business.

Franchise agreements tend to be for several years as the franchisee has to invest in marketing, staff training and sometimes real estate. Common examples of franchise businesses are McDonalds, Subway®, 7-Eleven®, Pizza Hut®, KFC® and Hertz®.

Q1. Does your company have any intellectual property suitable for a franchise model?

Q2. Have you invented a service that could be franchised?

Q3. Have you invented a business method that could be franchised?

Infrastructure Assets: Contracts

Many types of contracts are used in business and they are all infrastructure assets. Different types of contracts are industry specific. It might be an interesting exercise to make a list of each type of contract your business uses – you will be surprised by how many there are!

There is always the temptation to save money by copying a contract off the Internet and modifying it yourself. This is a bad idea.

Key contracts include employment contracts and getting these wrong can be a nasty and costly experience. Employee contracts should always have IP assignment clauses in them so that the company, not the employee, owns the IP. There are several different types of employment contracts.

Other key contracts are sales contracts, subcontractor contracts, shareholder agreements, non-executive director contracts, collaboration agreements, IP assignments and research contracts.

Signing up to badly-drafted or one-sided contracts (or even worse, not having contracts at all) is a bad idea because, firstly, you will be at a disadvantage in the event of a dispute and, secondly, for that reason potential investors and M&A partners will be deterred. Contracts which reveal an over-reliance on a single key customer or supplier also set off warning bells.

Q1. How many contracts does your company regularly use?

Q2. Are staff appropriately educated in the nature and use of contracts?

Q3. Would it be useful to have some employee lunchtime seminars on various legal contracts? Maybe your legal advisors would pop in to do that for free?

Infrastructure Assets: Search Engine Optimisation

Search engine optimisation, or SEO, is an umbrella term for the methods used to ensure the visibility of your web site and its content on search engine results pages (SERPs). The goal is to ensure that your web site pops up in the first five results of an unpaid search.

A strong site architecture with clear navigation will help search engines index your site quickly. More importantly, this will also provide visitors to your web site with a good user experience, (UX) and encourage repeat visits. Good UX is key, and is helped by regular updates and having videos on the site.

If not, there are companies that will overhaul your site and make it SEO friendly. The site should also have an SSL security certificate so that your site is https:// and shows the trusted padlock icon when visitors navigate to it.

SEO typically takes 3 to 6 months to show results.

Q1. Do you know how effective your web site is at generating prospects?

Q2. Is your web site more than 3 years old?

Q3. Should you get your web site SEO audited?

Infrastructure Assets: Social Media Dashboards

Social media dashboards (SMD) are systems that provide a one-stop shop for managing multiple social media channels. They input all the feeds from your social media platforms, such as Google+, LinkedIn, Facebook, Twitter and so forth. They enable you to have one source of output so you don't have to post to each platform you're on one platform at a time.

The SMD will enable people to have different levels of access to different social media platforms, but in a business context, you would typically have one person in charge of all social media so the corporate 'voice' is consistent.

SMDs enable content to be scheduled in advance, so you can, for instance, set up a week's content in one day and set it to upload over the next seven days.

Dashboards provide analytics so you can see which posts were popular and which did not work very well. Your evangelists are also notified so you can see who is retweeting or forwarding your content by geography.

Q1. Do you have an integrated social media strategy?

Q2. How frequently do you get updates from sites?

Q3. How do you analyse what content is working and what isn't?

Chapter 4 Summary

1. Infrastructure assets are the skeleton that gives a company strength
2. Corporate culture is "the way we do things around here"
3. Identify critical knowledge functions in a company
4. Document explicit knowledge
5. Identify required standards
6. Ensure IT systems are fit for purpose, especially legacy systems
7. Get great advisors on your Board
8. Ensure you always have good investor relations
9. Document business and management processes, update them regularly
10. Design a patent audit procedure with your patent attorney
11. Keep distributors motivated to sell your products not someone else's
12. Track royalty payments as they are usually underpaid
13. List contracts used by your company

Chapter 5

Introducing Human Centred Assets

Human centred assets are the assets a company has access to through its employees, subcontractors and associates. Of course, the company does not 'own' these people, but it can own the work they do as a result of their employment and subcontractor contracts.

The company has access to tacit human centred assets by benefitting from employee knowledge, creativity, memory and the enthusiasm employees have for the company. Other assets that should be considered include leadership, management and entrepreneurial qualities.

Human centred assets also include corporate memory, the accumulated knowledge of people who have been in the business over many years. Certain individuals act as 'gate-keepers' to historical data, having information and knowledge that is not necessarily written down anywhere. They are corporate historians. Building a corporate memory, together with knowledge management processes, will add value to the business. Knowing how knowledge flows in the organisation can be illuminating, and also helps to identify the gate-keepers.

You are always vulnerable to losing key employees and you can mitigate the damage this causes by putting restrictions in their contracts limiting their ability to take company information, staff and customers with them with they leave. However, if those restrictions are too onerous the courts may judge them unenforceable so you should always take legal advice on this. Your best protection is to run a great company and a "happy ship" – good people will want to join you and stick around.

Human Centred Assets: Work Related Competencies

The individual in the workplace is a huge secret. When hiring, we put a job specification in an advertisement and typically the applicant will re-write their résumé to fit the position. So when we hire someone, we are probably looking at a fraction of the talent of the individual instead of the whole person.

Employees in the UK frequently have what we call NVQ (National Vocational Qualifications), which aim to prepare them for a particular function in the work place. Sometimes these are useful, but it's hard to know what they mean unless you look at the curriculum, and who has time to do that?

Rather than pigeon-holing employees into 'jobs', maybe it's better to look at the whole person, their likes, dislikes, hobbies and so forth, and list their key competencies which are transferrable to the workplace.

> **Q1. Get team members to write a list of what they can do in life, each line starting with 'Annie can….'**

> **Q2. Regularly audit the competencies required for a job and look to see if the person doing that job has them.**

Q3. Ask team members what new competencies they think they could acquire to do a better job.

Human Centred Assets: Work Related Knowledge

Work related knowledge can be split into two categories, explicit and tacit. Explicit knowledge is knowledge that is or can be written down. Frequently it isn't written down, but the point is that it could be documented, presented and taught to other people.

Tacit knowledge is hard to quantify and hard to write down. This type of knowledge is frequently sensory, so it might be knowledge relating to design, music or even the way something looks.

Experts use tacit knowledge. Consider a mechanic who went to college to learn how to fix engines, but now he never uses the manuals and can tell what's wrong with an engine by the way it sounds.

Work related knowledge should be identified and documented or it could be lost forever. Since it's impossible to record all knowledge, it is best to identify critical knowledge functions, document them, and have a programme of apprenticeship to pass knowledge on to new generations.

Q1. How much does the business rely on tacit knowledge?
Q2. What can and should be made explicit?

Q3. How vulnerable is the business to particular people leaving?

Human Centred Assets: Corporate Memory

Corporate memory, sometimes called organisational memory, is the body of knowledge, information and data that is accumulated by an organisation over its life. Organisations that have been around for a while can easily forget what they have learnt over the years. Sometimes patents are rejected only for the business to discover that the 'prior art' was actually developed by themselves years before.

This is loss of corporate memory. Consider maintaining a really old airplane. The designers are long gone and the manuals lost – yet someone remembers an old photograph of this plane with its wings removed, and this is the only clue to the maintenance problem. Years ago, an inventor in a large UK chemical company was killed in a car accident and it took the company years to recover his lost knowledge.

Certain individuals may be the holders and gate-keepers of your corporate memory. As we increasingly become a knowledge economy, knowledge becomes a more precious asset, and individuals must be encouraged not only to grow corporate memory, but to share it.

Q1. Who are your custodians of corporate memory?

Q2. What will happen when they leave?

Q3. What are the critical knowledge functions of the business?

Human Centred Assets: Creativity

How do you harness creativity in the business? There are several methods that can be used in a team scenario to generate creative input that will produce innovative thinking, ideas for marketing campaigns and more.

Hire an expert to run a creative workshop or use some of the tools that are on the market, such as the Creative Whack pack or Edward de Bono's Six Thinking Hats, which has been around for years but is still really effective. Get everyone to read the paperback and role-play according to the rules. It's cheap and cheerful!

Another strategy is to mix up the skill sets. If there is an engineering problem to solve, don't just invite engineers to work on it. People from different disciplines won't be bogged down with the same belief models. Be prepared to throw stuff out of the window and start over.

Consider having a Corporate Jester to shock your business into new behaviour. Have no sacred cows. Think the unthinkable and do the undoable – no idea is too silly to consider.

Q1. How can you introduce more creativity into your company?

Q2. Who could be your Corporate Jester?

Q3. What sacred cows can be challenged?

Human Centred Assets: Passion

Most of us have to go to work to earn a living. Yet how many of us are passionate about our jobs? People who are passionate about their jobs are very valuable employees and they also have more fun at work!

Passion is infective. If a sales person is truly passionate about his company and its products, the prospect just might get infected too and buy.

When Apple first introduced the Macintosh in the 1980s, they also introduced the job title of 'Evangelist'. These were employees who were passionate about the Mac and were cheerleaders for this new way of doing things, encouraging people to 'Think Different'. They travelled the globe presenting and speaking to almost any audience they could get in front of. They were, and still are, passionate about Apple, its products, its technology and its culture.

Passionate employees believe body and soul in what they are doing. No belief, no passion. If management is not passionate, how can employees be passionate?

Q1. Do a passion audit in your company. Consider making it anonymous.

Q2 Ask key management how passionate they are about the company.

Q3. Consider some coaching to bring out the passion in employees.

Chapter 5 Summary

1. Human centred assets are assets a company has by way of its employees
2. Try to get a rounded picture of employees outside of the pigeon hole of their job
3. Knowledge can be explicit or tacit
4. Explicit knowledge can be written down tacit knowledge tends to be hard to document and is frequently sensory
5. Experts use tacit knowledge
6. Identify critical knowledge functions
7. Who are the gate keepers and corporate historians in your company
8. Find ways to stimulate creativity in your company
9. Is the management team passionate about the company?

Now you have a general idea of the nature of intangible assets we will be using in our Dream Ticket® process let's look at how you can begin to build your Dream Ticket®.

Chapter 6

Business Visualisation

When I moved from the UK to Silicon Valley in the mid 80's I embraced everything Californian. I loved the "alternate" Californian culture and delved into numerology, astrology, reflexology, reiki driving convertibles you name it.

One day I was asked to fly to Boston to see a client who was about to launch the first radio-based restaurant management system in the USA. There had been considerable disagreement in the product team about exactly what the system's features and benefits were and we went through the painful process of my typing the datasheet whilst the CEO, marketing and the technical team squabbled behind me over what I should type, sentence by sentence. After a period of several hours, we had the first draft of a data sheet that the team reluctantly agreed we were bringing to market.

A couple of weeks later the CEO decided he wanted the entire suite of product and corporate literature written over a weekend ready for a pre-launch event early the following week and requested I go back to Boston immediately to undertake the task.

Now I did not like writing! This was an assignment I really did not want and I complained bitterly to my boss Carolyn that I did not like writing and could not do the task. She ignored my protestations, slapped a paperback book into my hand and said: "Read this on the plane and you will be fine".

So I was sent back to Boston to sit in a hotel room and write around 6 documents ready for Monday morning. I had to be frog-marched to the plane door to make sure I actually went. (Airport security has changed a lot since then!!).

The paperback was called, *"Creative Visualisation"* written by Shakti Gawain in 1978.

Creative Visualisation is a process of getting what you want in life by visualising yourself as you would be when you had what you desired.

Shakti sets out four steps for creative visualisation

1. Set a goal
2. Create a very clear idea or picture
3. Focus on it often
4. Give it positive energy

The general idea is to "see" what you desired as if you already had it. This is supported by a set of affirmations, statements that you write down and say over an over that describe the situation <u>as if your goal had already been achieved</u>. So if you weighed 90 kilos and wanted to shed weight your affirmations might be:

"I love my body

I weigh 60 kilos

I look fabulous in my new bikini

My friends all tell me I look ten years younger

I naturally reach for healthy food options

I exercise every day"

You get the idea. You don't say "I *will* weigh 90 kilos, I *will* look 10 years younger when I lose weight" the affirmations are always in the future.

On the plane to Boston I read Creative Visualisation and wrote a list of affirmations aimed at changing my attitude toward writing.

"Writing is easy for me

The words just flow from my fingers

Writing is pure joy for me

It gives me so much pleasure to see my written work

I never get writers' block"

And so forth.

When I got to Boston I looked in the mirror and repeated my affirmations 5 times. Next morning before I started writing I said them another 5 times. Whenever I took a break I said them a couple more times and guess what? I finished all the documents by lunchtime on Sunday and I really enjoyed it! I am pleased to say that Creative Visualisation is still a best seller having sold millions of copies.

Jumping forward 20 years having identified intangible assets as key to my Intellectual Capital method I pondered if I could use these assets as strategic business tools? As we have already discussed building a business plan that predicts future business is hard to do.

So I wondered if you could use Creative Visualisation to "know" how a person or situation would be in the future, why couldn't you use Creative Visualisation to visualise to know" how a business would be in the future?

With a person you visualise the "situation" in the future, the attributes and situations thin, wealthy, happy, successful they are all adjectives, describing words.

So what are the "situations" or descriptions of the business that would become business affirmations? Yes, you are right, it's the status of the intangible assets as they would be in the future.

Business Visualisation (BIZVIZ®) is born!

Business Visualisation

To write a business plan that's achievable you have to "see and know" how the business would look in say 3 to 5 years in the future. This is hard to do because we have not "experienced" the future.

Consider driving from A to B. If you have never driven from Cambridge to London and you don't have a map you'd find it hard to get there — let alone describe "how" to get there. However, once you have driven there a few times you have the map in your head so it's easy to describe how to get there — that is unless you are my friend Toby who has no sense of direction.

Business visualisation is about seeing the business as it would be if it had achieved its corporate goals. The process involves choosing the set of assets that **would** be in place and in good shape when the business is successful. Once you have chosen the assets appropriate to your company and its goal you describe the situation each of the assets would be in when the business is successful. This is your Dream Ticket® and this is what the business aspires to.

When you know what success looks and feels like it's easy to make a plan to get there.

Chapter 6 Summary

1. Creative Visualisation is the process of getting what you desire in life by visualising yourself as if you already possessed it.
2. The four steps for creative visualisation are:
    a. Set a goal
    b. Create a very clear idea or picture
    c. Focus on it often
    d. Give it positive energy
3. Affirmations never include conditional words like "will, will be, when" but affirmative positive words like "is, have and am".
4. Business visualisation "BIZVIZ®" is the process of seeing how a business will look in the future when it's in a position to achieve its corporate goal.
5. The Dream Ticket® – is the list of intangible assets and their status as they will be when the business is in a position to achieve its corporate goal.
6. When you know what the future looks like it's easy to make a plan to get there.

Chapter 7

Introducing the Dream Ticket®

So what is a Dream Ticket®?

A Dream Ticket® is a set of affirmations related to the chosen set of assets such that when the affirmations are true, the business would have a clear shot, a home run, to achieve its business goals.

Affirmations are the most important part of creating the Dream Ticket®. Affirm means "to make firm"

An affirmation is a strong positive statement that something is already so. It's a way of making firm the state of the asset that you are visualising in the future.

What we are seeking to do is describe the business as it will be in the future when it had achieved its goal. The first 3 steps in the process to get a Dream Ticket® are:

1. Set the goal

2. Choose the assets the business will use to achieve its goal.

3. Describe the success scenario situation for each asset by way of an affirmation.

STEP 1: Choosing a Goal

As with creative visualisation business visualisation requires a goal. This is typically about revenues, market share, product adoption, it really doesn't matter but there are three rules about choosing the goal:

1. Choose a goal which is measurable
2. Choose a goal which is unambiguous
3. Choose a goal which has true meaning for the business

So choosing a goal such as "We have 100 haulage trucks" is measurable but may not be meaningful to the business unless they are occupied and working every day so the real goal is a revenue goal – the 100 trucks are the part of the means to achieve that goal.

Another example is "we are the de-facto standard" for testing for contamination in chickens. How will you measure that?

Questioning the Goal

Once you have chosen your goal ask yourself "Is this really the right goal?" Would the business be better off with a different goal? Exactly where did the goal come from?

Too often a goal is set by a Board or large Shareholder

"We will double revenues in the next twelve months"

"We will open a subsidiary in the USA this year"

"Once the company is re-financed it must do £2.3 million in its first year.

These are all goals I have seen handed down to a management team with little hope of success. Fortunately, now the Dream Ticket® methodology will provide management teams with clear information way in advance that will make it clear that such goals are unachievable with available resources.

STEP 2: Step into the Future – Choose your Assets

Take a look at the list of assets in the previous chapter. Ask yourself the same question of each one.

Does my business need this asset in order to be successful in 3 or 5 years?

So if your goal is $10 million in revenue within 3 years start with Markets Assets

1. Will the company need to have great product names?
2. Will the company need to have branding?
3. Will the company need to have "Positioning"?
4. Will the company need to have brand recognition?
5. Will the company need to have a tagline?
6. Will the company need to have a jingle?
7. Will the company need to have evangelists?
8. Will the company need to create tribes?

9. Will the company need to have endorsements?

You get the general idea so review each of the 46 assets in Chapter 2 reviewing market, intellectual property, infrastructure and human centred assets. You should finish up with around 25 assets in your Dream Ticket®.

In order to make the asset choosing process easier I have created the BIZVIZ® card deck. The BIZVIZ® card deck consists of 46 cards each describing the assets outlined in Chapter 2 together with an introductory card for each of the four categories. Taking each card read the text and place the cards in two piles: assets relevant to your goal and assets not relevant to your goal.

The BIZVIZ® card deck is available at www.magicmonkey.eu. And using it choosing the assets takes around 30 minutes.

From this point on we will be looking at some diagrams. If you don't have either the Dream Ticket® e-book or the paper version all of these diagrams can be downloaded from www.magicmonkey.eu/downloads .

In Figure 7.1 are the assets that were chosen by a new consulting company Brownbank whose goal is to generate £500k in revenue by the end of year 2. Looking at each of the categories you can see that market assets is the dominant category and this is not surprising as their greatest challenge is to create a market presence and get clients in order to hit the revenue goal. They decided they needed all of the market assets except taglines, jingles, hashtags, a distribution channel (as every employee carried a sales target), so in fact its direct sales. They did not need franchisees.

In the IP category, they decided they only needed copyright and trademarks.

In the Infrastructure asset category they decided that corporate culture and management philosophy were important to them as well as IT systems, management processes and everything to do with digital marketing.

From the human centred assets category, they chose work-related competencies and knowledge, creativity and passion.

This exercise resulted in an asset list of 28: 15 Market Assets, 2 intellectual property assets, 7 infrastructure assets and 4 human centred assets giving 28 in total.

If you have more than 25-30 assets you will need to be ruthless and go through the assets you have chosen asking the question:

"Is this asset essential to achieve our goal or is it a nice to have?" Then weed out the nice to have's.

Larger and well-established companies might have more assets but then they may also have more resources to support them. How to deal with having too many assets in the Dream Ticket® will be discussed later.

	ASSET	Relevant?
MARKET	Names	Y
	Brands	Y
	Positioning	Y
	Brand Recognition	Y
	Tag Lines	N
	Jingles	N
	Prospects, Customers and Evangelists	Y
	Tribes	Y
	Endorsements	Y
	Repeat Business	Y
	Backlog	Y
	Web Sites	Y
	High Click Through, Low Bounce	Y
	Digital Media Strategy	Y
	Hashtags	N
	On line Communities	Y
	Blogs	Y
	Videos	Y
	The Distribution Channel	N
	Franchisees	N
IP		
	Patents	N
	Copyright	Y
	Trade Secrets	N
	Trademarks	Y
	Design Rights	N
	Special IP Categories	N
INFRA-STRUCTURE	Corporate Culture	Y
	Knowledge Management	N
	Management Philosophy	Y
	Standards	N
	IT Systems	Y
	The Board	N
	Shareholder and Investor Relations	N
	Business and Management Processes	Y
	Patent Audit Procedures	N
	Distribution Agreements	N
	License Agreements	N
	Franchise Agreements	N
	Contracts	Y
	Optimised SEO	Y
	Social Media Dashboards	Y
HUMAN CENTERED	Work Related competencies	Y
	Work related knowledge	Y
	Corporate memory	N
	Creativity	Y
	Passion	Y

Figure 7.1 Brownbank Asset Choices

STEP 3: Live in the Future – Create the Affirmation

Some assets will be common to all businesses.

For example, take names. We know the business or product and service will have to have a name, but what kind of name? Who do we want that name to mean something to? Is it easy to spell? Is there a .com available? Can it be confused with any competitor's name?

Bear in mind that the affirmation is designed so that in the future it must be able to pass the "true" test.

Remember when you are designing your affirmations design them so they are measurable. Let's look at some examples.

Examples of Market Affirmations

In order to generate £10 million in revenues within 3 years "All our product names are easy to spell and remember"

In order to generate £10 million in revenues within 3 years "Our product name is trademarked"

In order to generate £10 million in revenues within 3 years *"Our product name works for us globally"*

Looking at the names "Google" or Yahoo these hit all three criteria above, more so they are alliterative so they roll off the tongue easily.

Let's look at brand recognition.

Having an affirmation that's

"We have great brand recognition" is not specific enough and cannot easily be tested to pass the "true test"

Who do you want to recognise your brand? If your product is aimed at dairy farmers then as prospects we want dairy farmers to recognise the brand and don't really care if the rest of the population recognises it or not. So the affirmation for brand recognition might be:

In order to generate £10 million in revenues within 3 years, "80% of dairy farmers recognise our brand".

However if our product is aimed at dairy farmers with large farms producing over a million gallons of milk a day then the affirmation must reflect that.

In order to generate £10 million in revenues within 3 years "80% of large dairy farmers recognise our brand"

Its best to get the affirmation as focussed as possible then it's easier to quantify which we will talk about later.

Also nailing down who we want to recognise the brand will help determine where to promote it. Farmer's Weekly, LinkedIn or Facebook?

Examples of Intellectual Property Affirmations

Patents: *In order to generate £10 million in revenues within 3 years "All our products are protected by at least 3 patents"*

Trade Marks: In order to generate £10 million in revenues within 3 years *"All our brands are protected with Trade Marks in key territories where we do business"*

Trade Secrets: In order to generate £10 million in revenues within 3 years *"Our products are protected by trade secrets which are kept by all employees"*. In this case you might want to talk about a specific trade secret.

Design Rights: In order to generate £10 million in revenues within 3 years" *Our products have design rights which makes them stand out from our competition"*

Examples of Infrastructure Affirmations

In order to generate £10 million in revenues within 3 years "We have a sales tracking system that reports on repeat business"

In order to generate £10 million in revenues within 3 years *"All medical products comply with the Medical Devices Directive"*

In order to generate £10 million in revenues within 3 *years "We have a "can-do" corporate culture that's embraced by all employees"*

In order to generate £10 million in revenues within 3 years *"Our IT systems are fit for purpose to support the business"*

In order to generate £10 million in revenues within 3 years *"Our business processes make selling and supporting our customers easy"*

Examples of Human-Centred Affirmations

In order to generate £10 million in revenues within 3 years, *"All critical knowledge functions in the company have been identified"*

Trade Secrets: In order to generate £10 million in revenues within 3 years *"Key employees are up to date with the latest FDA legislation"*

In order to generate £10 million in revenues within 3 years *"Tacit knowledge relating to trade secrets is shared"*

Below in Figure 7.2 is the Dream Ticket® for Brownbank whose goal is to generate £500k by the end of year 2. For future ease of reference, I have given each affirmation a short identifier. M meaning market, IP for intellectual property, I for infrastructure and H for human centred.

MARKET	ASSET	AFFIRMATIONS
M1	Names	We have memorable names for each of our services
M2	Brands	We have memorable brands for each of our services
M3	Positioning	4 out of 5 prospects are aligned with our Positioning statement
M4	Brand Recognition	80% of prospects recognise our brands
M5	Prospects, Customers and Evangelists	We have 20 evangelists who will refer our services
M6	Tribes	We have tribe of 500 followers on our Linked-In Group
M7	Endorsements	We have 20 endorsements on our web site and add another 5 each quarter
M8	Repeat Business	80% of our clients return to us for more services
M9	Backlog	We have 10 projects in backlog at all times
M10	Web Site	We have a web site that generates 100 new leads every year
M11	High Click Through, Low Bounce	40% of all visitors to our web site stay for > 1 minute
M12	Digital Media Strategy	Our web site is optimised for sales and lead generation
M13	On line Communities	We have communities in LinkedIn and facebook
M14	Blogs	We blog to our on-line community every week
M15	Videos	We have 4 videos on our web site explaining our services refreshed quarterly
IP		
IP1	Copyright	All our material is copyright
IP2	Trademarks	We have trademarks for our brands in the territories where we operate
INFRASTR		
I1	Corporate Culture	We have a family culture that makes us a cohesive team
I2	Management Philosophy	Our management philosophy is set out on the wall in every office
I3	IT Systems	Our IT systems have increased our productivity by 50%
I4	Business and Management Processes	We have documented business processes we always follow
I5	Contracts	We have minimal contracts so we are easy to work with
I6	Optimised SEO	Our web site is SEO we have an SEO audit every quarter
I7	Social Media Dashboards	We use Hootsuite to manage our social media effacacy
HUMAN		
H1	Work Related competencies	We have a list of work related competencies and all staff tick all boxes
H2	Work related knowledge	Our staff all have 3 years' experience in our sector
H3	Creativity	We are a highly creative team
H4	Passion	100% of our staff are passionate about the quality of the service we provide.

Figure 7.2 Brownbank Assets and Affirmations

We will use these identifiers in the future to track the progress of the affirmation relative to its goal.

As you can see in the above Dream Ticket® (Figure 7.2) the majority are measurable.

What's dominating the direction of the business?

Every company has its own unique Dream Ticket®. For example, a high technology company will probably have several affirmations that relate to intellectual property whereas a company selling consulting services may not have any IP assets at all other than trademarks.

Some companies will have many affirmations relating to infrastructure others will have few. The age of the company will also have an impact on the nature of assets. Established companies will have more infrastructure assets than start-ups as they will have existing systems whereas start-ups will have few if any infrastructure assets.

Refining and Focussing the Affirmation

I have seen many business plans where the forecast numbers assume a percentage of the total market. This most never works as the marketing efforts can't be targeted with such a broad goal.

Take for example the asset brand recognition. The people we want to recognise our brand and hopefully buy must be suspects and prospects to purchase our products and services, the rest we don't care about. But how many prospects do we need to recognise our brand in order to achieve forecast sales? 100%, 50%? Also, where are these prospects? To refine this affirmation you will need to look at two numbers:

1. The total market
2. The available market

If you are selling novel beach balls for £5 and your chosen distribution method is to have people selling your beach balls on the beach it's an impulse buy. The market size for your beach balls is probably huge. I don't know how many beaches there are in the world, probably thousands, so for ease let's say there are 10,000 beaches in the world and let's say that on average 1000 people visit these beaches once a year in the summer so the potential market is 10 million beach balls and £50 million.

However, if you are a 5 person company in the UK you cannot access the total market unless you recruit 1000 people to sell on the beaches. So the **available market** is the number of beaches where you have a person selling your beach balls. If you have 10 people selling beach balls in the south of England the available market is much smaller it is 10,000 not 10 million so £50,000. By focussing on brand recognition for the 10,000 in the south of England instead of the 10 million, not only will it be much cheaper but you would have a better chance of predicting how many beach balls you would sell. So the brand recognition needs to be related to the available market.

However not everyone in the available market will buy. Let's say 1 in 10 are buying today (you will have to ask your man on the beach to calculate his hit rate), so 10,000 beach balls at £5 each = £50,000.

So to double sales you would want say 50% of beachgoers in the South of England to recognise your brand as not everyone who recognises the brand will buy perhaps 2 out of 10 will?

Refining the affirmations so the mathematics stack up where possible is key and it will also provide a focus for the marketing efforts we are going to talk about shortly. The affirmation must describe the "situation" as it will be in the future such that the goal can be met.

Getting Goosebumps

Your Dream Ticket® is your shopping list of "situations" that you are going to create.

To test your affirmations there is no better way than to read them out loud. Vocalising is extremely important to this exercise. If you have built the Dream Ticket® as a team then the team should read the affirmations out loud together.

Hopefully, everyone will get very excited. Creating a Dream Ticket® is a fantastic team building exercise. Sometimes participants get goose bumps and quite exuberant and that's a good sign. After you have repeated your affirmations a few times the team should be comfortable. If you have any doubts about any of the affirmations keep repeating them for a bit longer. This exercise is supposed to be a stretch. If anyone in the team really can't see in their mind's eye the company achieving this affirmation, it won't. So tweak it until the team is comfortable with every affirmation. Or remove it. Banish any doubt.

Everyone needs to know it will happen.

Once you and your team are comfortable with your affirmations you have built your Dream Ticket®. The next step is to do a gap analysis.

Chapter 7 Summary

1. Affirmations "make firm" a future business scenario.
2. A Dream Ticket® is a set of affirmations related to the chosen set of assets such that when the affirmations are true the business should achieve its business goals.
3. A Dream Ticket® is made up of "affirmations" that describe the future status of intangible assets.
4. There are 3 steps in the process to get a Dream Ticket®.
    a. Set the goal
    b. Choose the assets the business will need to achieve its goal.
    c. Describe the success scenario situation for each asset by way of an affirmation.
5. Goals must be measurable
6. A Dream Ticket® normally has around 25 assets
7. Choosing the assets is easier with the BIZVIZ® card deck
8. When creating affirmations make sure they can be measured.
9. The age and nature of the business will affect the number and nature of affirmations.
10. The Dream Ticket® is the "shopping list" of situations you are going to create.
11. The team must "know" the affirmation is possible.

Chapter 8

Measuring Market Assets

Where would you rather be?

At the bottom of a mountain pushing a rock to the top, not able see what it's like at the top

Or

On top of the mountain looking back down able to see how you managed to get to the top?

In the previous chapter we went through the first three steps in making the future into a reality for Brownbank we:

STEP 1: Set the goal

STEP 2: Chose the assets we need to hit the £500k revenue goal

STEP 3: Characterise the future situation of each asset in our Dream Ticket® by way of an affirmation.

We also gave a short identifier to each asset M1, M2, IP1 and so forth. The reason for doing this is that in STEP 5 we are going to plot these assets on to a target so we can track them over time which will turn out to be a powerful and very visual way of looking at the company in a single view.

Next, we need to start to appraise the current situation.

STEP 4: Index Your Assets – look back to today

We are going to take a look at the status of each asset as it is today. We are seeking to index each asset so we can measure the gap. Our mission is to have a strong set of assets with each asset having an index of 5 out of 5 (meaning it is strong) 1 means that it is weak and requires work.

Depending on the nature of the asset you may have to break it down into sub-assets. For example, if one asset is IT infrastructure there will probably be some systems that are in great shape and others that could use improvement. It's up to you to choose a representation that enables you to have meaningful goals.

So how will you do this? Below there are eight methods for evaluating the strength of market assets.

Asset	Customer Survey	Customer Interview	Analyse Sales	Analyse Cost of sales	Market research	Audit Agreements	Competitive Analysis	SEO tools
Names	Y	Y			Y		Y	
Brands	Y	Y			Y		Y	
Positioning	Y	Y			Y		Y	
Brand Recognition	Y	Y			Y		Y	
Tag Lines	Y	Y			Y		Y	
Jingles	Y	Y			Y		Y	
Evangelists		Y	Y		Y			
Endorsements		Y	Y		Y			
Repeat Business	Y	Y	Y	Y	Y			
Backlog			Y		Y			
Web Sites	Y	Y	Y		Y		Y	Y
High Click, Low Bounce			Y		Y			Y
Digital Media Strategy	Y	Y	Y	Y	Y		Y	Y
Hashtags	Y	Y	Y	Y	Y			Y
Online Communities	Y	Y	Y		Y		Y	
Blogs	Y	Y	Y		Y		Y	Y
Videos	Y	Y	Y		Y		Y	
Distribution Channel	Y	Y	Y	Y	Y	Y	Y	
Franchisees	Y	Y	Y	Y	Y	Y	Y	

Figure 8.1 Methods for Evaluating Market Assets

Customer Survey

Customer Surveys are used to determine feedback to products, plans, people, support and more. Surveys unlike customer interviews, stick to a format so that responses can be used to compare apples to apples. Frequently customer surveys are outsourced to companies that specialise in this work. To be honest I don't really like them too much as whenever I am approached for feedback from a third party I automatically think "How come they could not be bothered to call me themselves?" so I feel negative about them. Surveys might make sense when a very large number of customer responses are required, but I prefer interviews as discussed below.

1. Customer Interviews

Of course, everyone knows we should talk to our customers regularly but I bet most of us don't. I have to be honest I don't do enough of this either, it's easy to get busy and forget. However, it's really so important to engage whilst actually asking for nothing in return. If the person contacting the customer is senior in the company then all the better, CEO is best. From time to time I admit I have been horrified at customer feedback to our sales efforts and sometimes have been on the receiving end of customers applauding changes in my sales and marketing team as they disliked them so much.

Not a good place to be.

Customers are a super easy and rich source of information on products and future plans which is why in the methods for evaluating market assets they are mentioned so regularly. Unlike a survey, interviews ought to encourage the customer to talk. I find its best to have some outlined questions but tend to use these as prompts rather than structure.

To get a good quality interview it's key to make sure that within the first 5 seconds of the call you manage the customer's expectation with reference to how much time you require and ask if it's convenient to talk now. If they are busy get off the phone fast! Even better ask for a phone appointment for a chat in advance.

2. Analyse sales

Analysing sales is useful to determine trends and where sales are coming from, direct, indirect or Internet. New market trends can be spotted by odd-looking customers buying from a market segment new to your business.

Find out what prompted sales? Did they watch videos or follow blogs and social media? What percentage of sales are repeat business? Surely the best possible type of sale?

3. Analyse Cost of Sales

How much are sales costing? What's the most effective channel? When a product or service is new it may well require a bag carrying sales person to make the sale. Once the product has traction perhaps a sale can be made via the company's web-site.

How much time is a sale taking? If a sale requires two or three visits before close that's costly unless the sale is of high value. Make sure sales staff are aware of the cost of a sales hour, a support hour and other expenses to close the sale, so that profits are not being eaten up due to poor time management.

4. Market Research

Market research is required for a large number of things but the key is to make sure that the "research" is always done in the context of *your* business. That's why I rarely purchase market research from professional research companies as they show general industry trends, not trends relating to "my" company.

Market research is essential to ensure that competitive analysis is accurate – a key tool for the sales force. Also when naming companies and products it's good to know what the names, taglines and jingles are for competitive products and services so that yours stand out. When I was running a medical devices/aesthetics business we used to go to trade shows and the corporate colours were a sea of powder blue and various flavours of green making it impossible for any company to stick out from the crowd. So we decided to back branding with unique colours and turned up at trade shows with a hot pink booth and branding. We also paid for hot pink footprints to lead delegates from the entrance right up to our booth. By the end of day one, everyone knew who we were "the pink people".

5. Audit Agreements

Auditing distribution and franchise agreements enable you to determine whether or not they are still suitable for the business and that you are getting what the company requires from franchisees and distributors. Keeping the distribution channel motivated to sell, should be a high priority so agreements may need to be modified to keep the relationship "fresh" and worthwhile for both parties.

6. Competitive Analysis

Looking at what the competition is up to on a regular basis will help to build strategies which differentiate you from the competition but also will help you see how you can out-manoeuvre them in the marketplace. Look at how they position themselves in the market against your products and services. I have already mentioned competitive analysis earlier but I would like to share my preferred way of doing product and service competitive analysis.

An example of how this will look is shown in Figure 8.2. So open up a spreadsheet.
1. In the left-most column add the title "Features"
2. For each competitor, you have add a column to the right with their name at the top.
3. In the right-most column add the name of your product
4. In the features column, add all the features of competitor 1

5. Then underneath add the features of competitor-2 which competitor -1 did not have, so they are not already on the list
6. Now add the features of all the other competitors that are not already on the list so you finish up with a combined list of all competitor features.
7. Now add any features your product has that are not already on the list
8. Next, populate all cells with YES or NO depending upon whether each competitor product and your product possess each feature.
9. Then sort the spreadsheet so that the where there is a "YES" in every row, these are at the top and so the "NO" cells drop to the bottom.

Where there is a YES in every column these features are probably mandatory, they are requirements for success, without them, the product would probably fail. For example, all smartphones need to have a camera.

Where there is a "YES" in a row and all the others all have a "NO" this might be a competitive advantage or it's a feature that's unnecessary.

Hopefully, your product will have a "YES" in every row and also have a number of "YES"s where your competition has "NO". These should be your USPs, your unique selling propositions. Ideally in your column you should have nothing but "YES".

Features	Comp 1	Comp 2	Comp 3	Comp 4	YOU
Comp 1 F1	Y	Y	Y	Y	Y
Comp 1 F2	Y	Y	Y	Y	Y
Comp 1 F3	Y	Y	Y	Y	Y
Comp 2 F1	☐	Y	Y	☐	Y
Comp 3 F1	☐	☐	Y	Y	Y
Comp 4 F1	☐	☐	☐	Y	Y
YOU F1	☐	☐	☐	☐	Y
YOU F2	☐	☐	☐	☐	Y
YOU F3	☐	☐	☐	☐	Y

FIGURE 8.2 Competitive Analysis 1

Finally, sort the spreadsheet so that your product is first under features and all of your USP's are at the top as shown in Figure 8.3. This exercise does take some time and research, but most of the data you require will be on your competitor's web sites. This is a must do exercise as not only is it a superb sales tool it should give you great insight into the competition.

Features	Comp 1	Comp 2	Comp 3	Comp 4	YOU
YOU F1	N	N	N	N	Y
YOU F2	N	N	N	N	Y
YOU F3	N	N	N	N	Y
Comp 1 F1	Y	Y	Y	Y	Y
Comp 1 F2	Y	Y	Y	Y	Y
Comp 1 F3	Y	Y	Y	Y	Y
Comp 2 F1	N	Y	Y	N	Y
Comp 3 F1	N	N	Y	Y	Y
Comp 4 F1	N	N	N	Y	Y

FIGURE 8.3 Competitive Analysis 2

In addition to product competitive analysis, look at the competition's outward facing marketing material such as web site, product names, their distribution channel and so forth which should also be on their web-site. What are they doing better than you? Can you copy to good effect any of their marketing ideas? Decide if you need to do a competitive analysis as just described for their web-site, channels and other market assets.

SEO Tools

This is a very fast moving sector and no doubt by the time I finish typing it will be out of date. Unless you are a large company able to afford a specialist digital marketing team my preferred way to keep on top of digital media strategy and its evaluation is to outsource it to companies that specialise in this area. Get them to provide you with regular analytics and advice on how to make your website more effective. At the time of writing, my favourite is Exposure Ninja which is a UK based company that has customers in most English speaking countries.

That said, you need to decide what the mission of your website is. For those of us who use Exposure Ninja it's definitely as a working sales engine. Too many companies treat their websites as an information only vehicle or an online magazine. Take a good hard look at your website and ask yourself what benefit does it bring to the business? How will it get your prospects to engage with you? How rigorous are you in analysing the effectiveness of your digital media strategy? Remember it's also an infrastructure asset as we have previously mentioned.

Chapter 8 Summary

1. Measure market assets so they can be ranked out of 5.
2. Measuring market assets will enable us to complete a gap analysis
3. Five is the top score 1 is the weakest
4. Customer surveys are useful when you require a large number of respondents

5. Customer interviews are the richest source of feedback on your products and services
6. Cost of sales should reflect the revenue from the product
7. Market research will help you determine how to position your product against the competition
8. Competitive analysis is essential to understand your USPs and also how you can out-manoeuvre the competition
9. Digital media is so important and fast-changing it should be done by specialists and possibly out-sourced.

Chapter 9

Methods for Evaluating IP Assets

I use seven methods to evaluate IP assets as outlined below.

Asset	Survey for Market Pull	Competitor Analysis	Audit Portfolio	ROI Legal Fees	Survey Knowhow	Survey Tacit Knowledge	Freedom to Operate
Patent	Y	Y	Y	Y	Y	Y	Y
Copyright	Y	Y	N	N	N	Y	N
Design Rights	Y	Y	Y	Y	N	N	N
Semiconductor Top Rights	Y	Y	Y	Y	Y	Y	N
Database Rights	Y	Y	Y	Y	Y	Y	N
Trade Secrets	Y	Y	N	N	Y	Y	N
Trade Marks	Y	Y	Y	Y	Y	Y	N

Figure 9.1 Methods for evaluating Intellectual Property Assets

Putting a specific value on Intellectual Property Assets (for example for a company sale or round of funding) is a specialist skill and you may need input from an IP valuation expert.

1. Survey for Market Pull

As with all assets their value increases if there is pull in the market. The value of a patent manifests in a variety of ways. It can protect a product (better if several patents (a thicket) protect one product) or it can be a revenue source in its own right if it is licensed. If you have just invented a totally biodegradable plastic bottle you may wish to consider if you can make more money keeping that invention to yourself for your products or licensing it to other interested parties.

Good patent attorney should always quiz you concerning the commercial prospects of a patent before agreeing to draft a patent application.

2. Competitive Analysis

Looking to see what IP competitors have, may influence your decision to file a patent or otherwise. Patent applications are written in a specific style, so it may be hard for the uninitiated to determine if a competitive patent has already been filed, but again a patent attorney can advise you. Whenever I think we have an idea for a potential patent before we start any development we run the idea past our patent attorney who gives advice on how we might modify the idea to make it patentable and stronger. Patent attorneys can also advise on how to avoid infringing an existing patent.

3. Audit Agreements & ROI on Legal Fees

I am putting these two methods together as they go hand in hand when managing an intellectual property portfolio. Patent renewal fees can get extremely expensive as the original patent turns into a family that gets filed in various countries. Fees for drafting and filing new patents range in price depending on the complexity of the patent which in turn determines how long it will take a patent attorney to draft it.

I recommend an IP audit with your patent attorney every twelve months to ask the following questions:

- What is the purpose of this patent?
- Is the patent protecting a product that is currently selling or will be sold in the future?
- Is the patent protecting the product in key territories?
- What is the ROI for a particular patent?
- Should this patent be dropped? Is it value for money?

4. Survey Know-how

This is an interesting topic and one that I have addressed in my book "Corporate Memory". Know-how is practical knowledge or perhaps a skill that employees have that is key to the business. Know-how might be how to service a piece of machinery, how to build a product, how to calibrate a piece of equipment, how to bake a certain type of cake and so forth. By surveying employees it's possible to discover "who knows what". If know-how is able to be written down it's explicit and can be shared with other members of the company. Knowhow can be confidential so that only your company is in possession of it. Then it should be protected as a trade secret. Trade secrets and patents go nicely hand in hand by limiting what's put into the public domain by way of a patent, and keeping key knowledge on its implementation in as a trade secret.

5. Survey Tacit Knowledge

Tacit knowledge is the opposite of explicit knowledge in that it cannot be written down. This type of knowledge tends to relate to creative skills and may be visual, auditory or tactile. In my early career I founded and ran an Artificial Intelligence Research laboratory for three years before moving to Silicon Valley. We won a contract to work with a major UK food company who wanted to formalise the way they invented a new low fat spread.

We met with their two key chemists with a view to capturing their knowledge so that it could be incorporated into an Expert System.

By way of explanation, they took me into the laboratory and gave me a list of ingredients to make a gallon of new margarine. I asked them what they did next. They replied they had a secret method for mixing the ingredients, then they:

1. Looked at the sheen on the top of the liquid and

2. Listened to the sound of the "glop" as the paddles mixed it.

Excited I asked what they did next.
They said they would scale up to 5 gallons and:
1. Look at the sheen on the top of the liquid
2. Listen to the sound of the "glop" as the paddles turned.

If these were satisfactory they scaled up again.

I asked what they would do if the mixture did not pass the sheen/glop test and they grinned at me and said: "Well we fiddle with the amounts of each ingredient and start over".

That was the end of that exercise for me. They had a good laugh at my expense!

I recommended an apprenticeship programme working with the two scientists so the apprentice "knew" what a good glop sounded like and could "see" what a good sheen was.

This type of situation is common when a person is an expert. They "know" when something sounds, looks or feels right and so knowing who these people are in the company is important for tacit knowledge retention.

6. Freedom to Operate

The last in my list of methods is to look at freedom to operate (FTO). This is an exercise that companies take prior to launching a product in a new territory to ensure that they will not be infringing someone else's patents or trademarks. Private law firms will undertake FTO for a fee. Where the product is going to be global an FTO search is going to be very costly but arguably not as expensive as a patent litigation cost. Of course, an FTP search is never going to be totally exhaustive as it's impossible to identify all potentially competitive patents in a sea of hundreds. If the market is large, focus on major competitor patents in key territories, taking into consideration their ability to finance legal proceedings should they discover you are infringing their IP.

Chapter 9 Summary

1. It's best to protect products with a thicket of patents.
2. Before you commence development work, consult with your patent attorney to design in features that may make your invention a stronger patent.
3. Audit your patent portfolio annually.
4. Identify tacit knowledge in the company and ensure you have the longevity of knowledge via an appropriate apprenticeship scheme or other knowledge sharing initiative.
5. Plan FTO before launching a product in a new territory.

Chapter 10

Measuring Infrastructure Assets

I mostly use five methods for measuring infrastructure assets each of which is described below.

Asset	Determine ROI	Fit for purpose?	Determine added value	Interview Customers	Interview Employees
Corporate Culture		Y	Y	Y	Y
Knowledge Management	Y	Y	Y		Y
Management Philosophy	Y	Y	Y	Y	Y
Standards	Y	Y	Y	Y	Y
IT Systems	Y	Y	Y	Y	Y

The Board	Y	Y	Y	Y	Y
Shareholder and Investor Relations	Y	Y	Y	Y	
Business and Management Processes	Y	Y	Y	Y	Y
Patent Audit Procedures	Y	Y	Y		Y
Distribution Agreements	Y	Y	Y	Y	Y
License Agreements	Y	Y	Y		
Franchise Agreements	Y	Y	Y		
Contracts	Y		Y		Y
Optimised SEO	Y	Y	Y	Y	Y
Social Media Dashboards	Y	Y	Y		Y

Figure 10.1 Measures for evaluating Infrastructure Assets

1. Determine ROI

Determining the ROI is the most common method used to evaluate the investment in most infrastructure assets. What does it cost to facilitate corporate infrastructure? Today many systems can be outsourced making them more cost-effective. Also, there are new software applications and apps to help streamline business processes. It may be possible to cut costs by using people signed into the gig economy. There are also SAAS (software as a service) platforms, for a range of business processes to include personal assistants, sales tracking, proposal writing, calendar management and many more. Older businesses may be using legacy systems that paid for themselves long ago, but that does not mean they should be used. In auditing intangible assets I have frequently come across processes that were initiated years previously to include updating databases and creating reports that now no-one ever bothers or needs to read.

2. Determine fit-for-purpose

Get the management team together and take a hard look at whether infrastructure assets are fit-for-purpose. This is an ongoing exercise, as the needs of the business change over time and infrastructure should mirror business needs. Infrastructure assets should be reviewed at least once a year. Also take a look at who does what relating to business processes. In particular look for what I call "job creep" where people designated to do function A are helping with functions B and C, and people designated to be responsible for B and C are helping out with functions D and E. It's like a daisy chain that supports duplication, confusion, communication problems "Oh I thought Alison had done that", and weak systems.

Finally look at whether the systems give appropriate support to the staff. Ask staff what could the company provide that would make them more efficient.

3. Determine Added Value

What is the added value of each infrastructure asset? What added-value does the Board bring?

What is the corporate culture and is it beneficial to the business? I recently had lunch with a colleague whose company provides free meals 3 times a day, free bicycle fixing, massages and much more. He did add that whenever members of his team took advantage of the free evening meal they felt guilty and stayed to work an extra hour or so, making their work day 12 hours and frequently more. Is this a desirable lifestyle for your employees?

When I worked in Silicon Valley I found myself competing with colleagues to be first in in the morning and last out each night which just finished up with burn out.

Conversely, I have also had employees take advantage of flexi time, one even boasting to colleagues that they set alarms when "working" from home to tell themselves to send a few emails so it looked like they were working when they in fact, they were having a nice snooze.

4. Interview Customers

Ask your customers how easy it is to work with your company? Do you need all of the legal contracts you currently use? Are service and support agreements helpful to the business or do they work against it? Do you regularly audit distribution contracts? Have customers ever had any communication with any members of the Board, the Chairman in particular.

I used to have a consulting company called The Technology Broker that licensed IP taking a percentage of the revenue. I asked a local lawyer to draft an appropriate agreement for me. Unfortunately, it was very long and none of my prospective clients understood it. It was a major barrier to business for me until I stopped using it replacing it with a shorter easy to understand contract.

5. Interview Employees

Talk to employees about how they think the business could benefit from change. Encourage employees to be creative and participate in growing and modifying business processes. Is the management philosophy conducive to productivity? I once interviewed a senior salesperson who wanted to change jobs because he was expected to be sitting at his desk from 9 to 5 every day. Odd I would have thought he should be out with his customers!

Chapter 10 Summary

1. Are the systems in the company generating ROI, could any be better outsourced?
2. Do your systems add value to the business or do you use them because you always have?
3. Do your systems enable you to easily engage with customers?
4. Ask employees to design systems that would enable them to be more productive and give better quality information about the business.

Chapter 11

Methods for Evaluating

Human Centred Assets

Lastly, we are going to talk about how to measure human centred assets and as I am sure you will realise this can be challenging, but sometimes lots of fun! Figure 11.1 below shows a table of six ways to evaluate human centred assets. There are many more

1. Interview

We have already mentioned interviewing employees in the context of getting their opinion on the effectiveness of business systems, however here we are talking about interviewing employees to get a rounded picture of the individual. Who is that person you work with every day?

One way of doing this is to document work-related competencies. What undiscovered knowledge and skills does this person have that the business might benefit from.

Build a "can do" list with each employee beginning with the employee's name followed by "can":

Annie can write marketing plans

Annie can bring a product to market

Annie can write business literature

Annie can plan and manage projects

Asset	Interview	Test and assess	Knowledge Elicitation	Self-Assessment	Manager Assessment	Peer Review
Work-related competencies	Y	Y	Y	Y	Y	Y
Work-related knowledge	Y	Y	Y	Y	Y	Y
Corporate memory	Y		Y		Y	
Creativity	Y	Y			Y	Y
Passion		Y		Y	Y	Y

Figure 11.1 Measures for Evaluating Human Centred Assets

And so forth. You may have to help them as some people find it hard to talk about themselves whereas for others it's their favourite topic of conversation!

Sometimes in a team scenario, we play a game called "What you don't know about me"

In turn, each employee says:

"Something you don't know about me is that......... Encourage everyone to include anything they like – especially relating to hobbies.

Mostly this game is very entertaining and enlightening, but be prepared for some shocks!

I have unearthed tons of talent in all sorts of areas with colleagues that had some special skills invisible to me in the workplace.

Skills in running classic car rallies (Ah! a logistics person)

Painting (Ah! – she has a flair for design)

Writing poetry (possibly a good copywriter?)

And so forth.

Round the interview off with:

"If you could do anything in this company you are not currently doing what would that be?"

I used to be an academic teaching Computer Science at South Bank University (previously South Bank Polytechnic). A brand new computer lab with around thirty workstations had just been installed. Being short of cash during the summer vacation I volunteered to teach a group of around 20 ethnic minority underprovided teenage girls from London, who came to the Poly to get a taster of different occupations they might pursue.

They spent a day in the college bakery, a day in a laboratory and so forth. I volunteered to give them a day of computing and decided to find a way to teach them computer programming in a day. No small feat!

I found a piece of software called *"Karel the Robot"* which provided an environment for the girls to program a robot in a matrix world. There were only five instructions such as walking forward turning left, moving and putting a beeper down and picking it up. Karel could not turn right so had to turn left three times to turn right.

Some of the girls were challenged to distinguish left from right. So we practised being a robot walking around the lab turning left, making a right turn, putting a beeper down and picking it up. We mimicked a robot walk and were having a great time when the laboratory door opened.

Expecting to find the computer lab empty the Polytechnic Director Dr. John Beishon walked in with a visitor and was understandably shocked to find me walking around the lab with a bunch of young girls mimicking a robot turning left and right. He walked up to me and asked me what I was doing?

"Teaching these girls computer programming Sir" I replied. He look at me as if I was nuts and they left.

A couple of hours later he returned alone to quiz me more and joined in helping with the girls. A week later I received a lunch invitation from Dr. Beishon who asked me what I thought about the teaching of computer science at the Polytechnic. I spoke freely and told him we ought to be teaching skills that would help the students get jobs quicker. I also said we also ought to be conducting research into Artificial Intelligence, which had become my all-consuming passion – (albeit I was not qualified to pursue it). Boldly, I added that we should be teaching AI as part of the curriculum which the universities were doing.

A week later I received another lunch invitation from Dr. Beishon which culminated in this conversation:

Dr Beishon "Well Annie I have been thinking about our conversation and I have decided we will have an AI research laboratory at the Poly".

Annie "Oh great, who will run it?"

Dr. Beishon "You will. I will relieve you of 50% of your teaching load. You can have the old office under the stairs on the first floor. I will pay for one research assistant and you can have the old accounting computer. If you want any more funding then you will have to go out and find it yourself". This arrangement will be for 1 year only.

I was floored.

So the Knowledge Based Systems Centre began, and in less than a year we won a huge 3 year grant "A Methodology for the Design of Knowledge Based Systems" from the European Commission's Esprit Programme. This enabled us to grow the unit to twenty or so staff and provided me with the funds to "buy myself out" of my teaching commitment.

The year was 1982.

Dr. Beishon was an extraordinary leader in the academic world and as I later learnt was famous for his "SAS management style" (*source The Guardian*). I was neither the first, nor last employee he chose to give an extraordinary opportunity to do something great. Thank you Dr B.

How would it be if every CEO, every year picked an employee and gave them the opportunity to do something really huge? A really big stretch?

2. Test and assess

There is a myriad of tests you can use to ferret out the personality types and potentialities of employees. Still popular is the Myers-Briggs test conceived in the 1940's, DISC assessment which evaluates behaviour focussing on the traits of dominance, inducement, submission and compliance. Others examine career success and happiness, humility, emotion, extraversion, agreeableness consciousness and so forth. When shared these are helpful to team building and understanding team dynamics.

3. Knowledge Elicitation

Knowledge elicitation is a technique that's used to gather knowledge that is typically unique to a couple of individuals and document it so it can be stored and shared. It can be a very long process (I spent 3 months with 1 individual in Italy who had unique knowledge of the process of designing the exterior of a nuclear reactor using an ancient piece of legacy computer code). He was about the last alive who could use it.

As previously mentioned it's not always possible to turn tacit knowledge into explicit knowledge so when this is the case its key to know who is in possession of key tacit knowledge and make sure you keep them and assign an apprentice to give their knowledge longevity.

This type of situation is common when a person is an expert. They "know" when something sounds, looks or feels right and so knowing who these people are in the company is important for know-how retention.

4. Self-Assessment, Manager Assessment and Peer Review

I have bundled these three techniques as basically they use the same evaluation questionnaire format from three different aspects yourself, your manager and your colleagues. Then the information is shared in a group meeting.

Chapter 11 Summary

1. Interview employees to find untapped knowledge that may be useful to the business
2. Pick individuals in the company you think may have talent and unleash it
3. Use psychometric testing to help build cohesive teams
4. Identify critical knowledge and document it wherever possible
5. Key tacit knowledge should be shared and transferred wherever possible with apprenticeship programmes

Chapter 12

Bringing the Dream Ticket® to Life

In this chapter I refer to 10 diagrams as Dream Ticket® is very visual, so if you would like larger diagrams these can be downloaded from www.magicmonkey.eu/downloads.

In the previous four chapters, I have suggested some ways which you might choose to measure and evaluate each of the assets in the Dream Ticket®. As I am sure you can imagine you can spend a huge amount of time and money on this activity and it's certainly not my suggestion that you do that. You might want to have a mix of formal measures or projects to rank each asset or you may wish to include some workshop evaluation that we will talk about in the next section.

The point of the index is to set a stake in the ground from where you can decide how best to grow the assets and plan your future.

Back to Brownbank our consulting company. You will see from the table in Figure 12.1 that having added the affirmations for each asset there is now an index. Where the asset is obviously very weak as perhaps before we started this process it was not on Brownbank's "to do list" I have suggested they don't waste time trying to calculate an accurate index. Give it a 1 and move on.

The next thing we are going to do it to plot Brownbank's assets on a target so we can visualise them in a single view.

MARKET	ASSET	AFFIRMATION	INDEX
M1	Names	We have memorable names for each of our services	5
M2	Brands	We have memorable brands for each of our services	5
M3	Positioning	4/5 prospects align with our Positioning statement	1+
M4	Brand Recognition	80% of prospects recognise our brands	1+
M5	Evengelists	We have 20 evangelists who will refer our services	1+
M6	Tribes	We have tribe of 500 followers on Linked-In Group	1
M7	Endorsements	We have 20 endorsements on our web site	1+
M8	Repeat Business	80% of our clients return to us for more services	1
M9	Backlog	We have 50 quarterly client reviews in backlog each year	1
M10	Web Site	We have a web site that generates 100 new leads every year	1+
M11	High Click Through, Low Bounce	40% of all visitors to our web site stay for > 1 minute	3+
M12	Digital Media Strategy	Our web site is optimised for sales and lead generation	5
M13	On line Communities	We have 500 members in our LinkedIn Group	1
M14	Blogs	We blog to our on-line community every week	1+
M15	Videos	We have 4 videos on our web site explaining our services	1
IP			
IP1	Copyright	All our material is copyright	5
IP2	Trademarks	We have trademarks for our brands in relevant territories	5
INFRASTR			
I1	Corporate Culture	We have a family culture that makes us a cohesive team	5
I2	Management Philosophy	Our management philosophy is widely displayed	4+
I3	IT Systems	Our IT systems have increased our productivity by 50%	1+
I4	Bus and Man Processes	We follow documented business processes	1+
I5	Contracts	We have minimal contracts so we are easy to work with	5
I6	Optimised SEO	Our web site is SEO we have an SEO audit every quarter	5
I7	Social Media Dashboards	We use Hootsuite to manage our social media effacacy	1
HUMAN			
H1	Work Related competencies	All staff tick all competencies boxes	5
H2	Work related knowledge	Our staff all have 3 years' experience in our sector	5
H3	Creativity	We are a highly creative team	5
H4	Passion	100% of our staff are passionate about quality	5

Figure 12.1 Brownbank Indexed Dream Ticket®

The Target

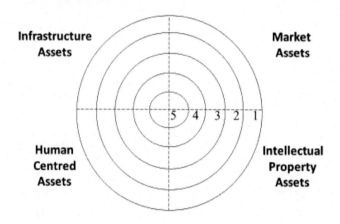

Infrastructure Assets

Market Assets

Human Centred Assets

Intellectual Property Assets

5 4 3 2 1

FIGURE 12.2 The Target and its four quadrants

STEP 5

5: Plot the Dream Ticket®

Figure 12.2 is the target we are going to use to plot the Dream Ticket®. As you can see the target is split into four quadrants mirroring the four categories of assets and the circles are numbered from 1 on the outside to 5 in the middle. It looks like an archer's target where the archer aims for the bullseye. That's exactly what we are going to do, aim to strengthen all our assets so they index at 5 and shoot into the middle of the target. As each asset has a unique identifier it can be plotted onto the target as a dot. The weakest assets will be plotted on the outside and the strongest will be in the middle.

It's the goal to move all the assets into the middle of the target over the allotted period. Where there is an arrow on the dot it means the asset is travelling in the direction the arrow is pointing, it's either getting stronger or weaker. Where there is no arrow it means it's stuck for some reason and so it might need some attention.

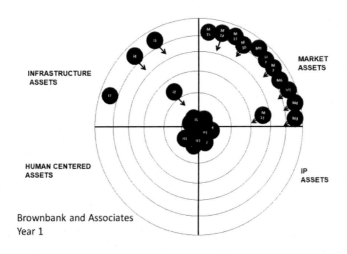

FIGURE 12.3 Brownbank Year 1 Target

Take a look at the target in Figure 12.3. As I mentioned it's a new consulting company and the position of the assets reflects that. There are more market assets than in any other category. This is not surprising as a new company has a lot of work to do to establish its place in the market. There are two strong market assets in M1 and M2 as this company has done a lot of work on branding and that's mirrored in the intellectual property assets where there are strong trademarks that protect the brands. M5 the website is strong as the company chose a market leader in web building where SEO was built in from day 1. The rest of the market assets are weak with a couple getting stronger. That's because this start-up has limited funds to invest in marketing and right now their target market is unaware of its existence.

Copyright is important to this company and it makes sure that all documents are clearly marked as it writes business books and software.

The infrastructure assets are in good shape for a new company. You would expect the team to share corporate culture and philosophy but the other infrastructure assets are weak, their systems for example. In a mature company this would be a bad thing but in a new company, it's always the case as they haven't had time to design and implement systems.

All the human assets are strong and this is important for a consulting company as they are selling people skills. In addition, if the company is new and the human centred assets are weak that would not be good. New companies need excellent people talent.

In summary, this is not a bad chart for a start-up. Typically you would expect market and infrastructure assets to be weak. Human Centred assets should always be strong. If the company was a high-tech start-up you would expect to see strong intellectual property assets.

Consider a different Dream Ticket® in Figure 12.4 and its target 1n 12.5. This is an eight-year-old high technology company ScanCo that sold a skin cancer scanner. As this company was in a state of flux we decided to add a zero circle so the indices go from 0 to 5. This is because the company did not even know, that most of assets it needed were actually required.

ScanCo has a lot more assets than Brownbank as it was doing R&D into skin cancer, generating patentable IP and also manufacturing a product in-house. In 2003 ScanCo was 5 years old and had 38 assets on its chart. See Figure 12.4

Let me quickly summarise ScanCo's indices

Of the 14 market assets, all are zero except three which are all ranked as one

Of the 9 infrastructure assets, two are zero, six are one and one is a two

Of the 6 IP assets, there are four zeros, one, one and one four

Of the 9 human centred assets, there is one zero, five ones and two twos.

In summary, almost everything is very weak and on the outside of the target.

		ScanCo Dream Ticket 2003	
MARKET			**INDEX**
	M1	Every Dermatologist recognises the Corporate brand	1+
	M2	Every Dermatologist recognises the Scanner brand	1+
	M3	Researchers in all related areas recognise the ScanCo name and brand	0
	M4	ScanCo is clearly positioned against all its major competitors	0
	M5	All Dermatologists in Europe, Australia and USA use ScanCo products	0+
	M6	All distribution contracts are monitored quarterly with feedback	0
	M7	The ScanCo website is the primary education site	0
	M8	ScanCo's advisory committees are comprised of world class members	0
	M9	ScanCo communicates regularly with its advisory committees	0
	M10	ScanCo has advisory panels for different market sectors	0
	M11	ScanCo has reimbursement codes for all USA products	0
	M12	ScanCo corporate literature is market sector focussed and informative	0
	M13	ScanCo has a world class training package, also available on the web	0
	M14	ScanCo sales are doubling each year	1+
INFRASTR			
	I1	Manufacturing is outsourced	1+
	I2	The product production cost has been reduced by 20%	0
	I3	The manufacturing process is fully documented	1+
	I4	All ScanCo products are ISO and GMP certified	1
	I5	ScanCo communicates to a content shareholder base every quarter	1
	I6	ScanCo has an informed and responsive telephone interface	1
	I7	Engineering projects are planned and execute to schedule	2+
	I8	All ScanCo products are rigorously tested	0
	I9	That ScanCo is financially Stable for 12 months	1
IP			
	IP1	All key IP at ScanCo is patented	4
	IP2	Every ScanCo product is protected by more than 3 patents	1
	IP3	Only patents that contribute revenue are filed and maintained	0
	IP4	Every patent generates ROI within 3 years	0
	IP5	ScanCo software is patented	0
	IP6	The company has a clear IP strategy	0
HUMAN			
	H1	ScanCo has a strong software department	1+
	H2	ScanCo has a management team that works well together	2+
	H3	Every employee understands how a scannerscope works	1
	H4	Every employee is able to forward a query call correctly	1
	H5	All employees can demonstrate the scannerscope	1
	H6	Diagnostic expertise is documented	0
	H7	All knowledge relating to manufacture and repair is documented	2
	H8	Key employees are motivated and are happy to work at ScanCo	2
	H9	The company is not reliant on knowledge assets of any one person	1+

FIGURE 12.4 ScanCo Dream Ticket® 2003 (previous page)

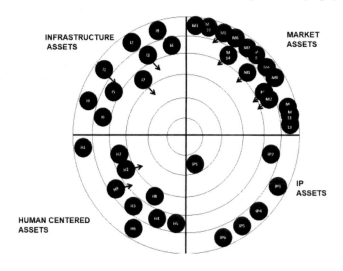

FIGURE 12.5 ScanCo Target 2003

What is very interesting about this Target is that human centred assets are in bad shape. The reason for this is that in its early years ScanCo's product was a very large (taller than a person) skin cancer scanner that looked like a robot so the employees were mostly engineers. However, the "cleverness" in the product offering was in its mathematical modelling of the skin and its software, not hardware. The company was behaving like a hardware company when it was really a software company. So at this time, ScanCo had only one software engineer with little experience of commercial software and many hardware engineers. Wrong way around. Two years later there were 10 software engineers and the manufacturing cost of the product had been slashed from £3000 to £300 and outsourced.

Also, look at infrastructure assets. For a five-year-old company it did not have the infrastructure it should have had as it was still "behaving" like a start-up when it should have transitioned into a more mature company. In particular, for a venture-backed company, it has two key assets in very poor shape I5 shareholder relations and I9 Financial stability, both very weak.

STEP 6: Choose measures that will close the gap

During this phase, we will look at each of the assets and choose a measure that should move the assets toward the centre of the target.

ASSET	INDEX	MEASURE
MARKET		
M1	5	No action monitor
M2	5	No action monitor
M3	1+	For 30 days ask prospects what pops into their head when they hear our "name"
M4	1+	Ask 50 suspects if they recognise your brand
M5	1+	Approach customers for a satisfaction ranking then propose evangelism
M6	1	Blog weekly to the group
M7	1+	Approach customers asking for an endorsement
M8	1	Ask accounts to keep a historical customer log
M9	1	Measure for M10 should impact this
M10	1+	Ramp up on-line marketing. Make sure web site is on all documentation
M11	3+	Check weekly Analytics reports. Use Blogs in M6 on web site
M12	5	have the web site audited quarterly
M13	1	Measure for M6 should impact this
M14	1+	Measure for M6 should impact this
M15	1	Make four 2 minute videos
IP		
IP1	5	No action monitor
IP2	5	No action monitor
INFRASTR		
I1	5	No action monitor
I2	4+	No action monitor
I3	1+	Do an audit of IT systems ranking out of 5 for fit-for-purpose
I4	1+	Do an audit of business processes ranking ouit of 5 for fit-for-purpose
I5	5	No action monitor
I6	5	No action monitor
I7	1	Decide to trial Hootsuite
HUMAN		
H1	5	No action monitor
H2	5	No action monitor
H3	5	No action monitor
H4	5	No action monitor

FIGURE 12.6 Brownbank Measures

Looking at figure 12.6 Brownbank measures you can see they have a lot of work to do, mostly marketing. As you look at your list of measures you might think that it's looking like a huge amount of work and cost. Don't worry about that at this point.

Looking at the measures the most important issues for Brownbank are related to business generation: positioning, brand recognition, evangelists, lack of repeat business, lead generation, pretty much what you'd expect in a new consulting company. So their action list is:

M3 a 30-day positioning exercise

M4 a 50 person brand recognition exercise

M5 a programme to locate evangelists

M6 a blogging campaign

M7 an endorsement campaign

M8 start a repeat business tracking log with their accounts department

M10, 11 and 12 a website review and digital marketing review

M15 make 4 videos

I3 and I4– look to see if IT and business systems are fit for purpose

I7 do a Hootsuite trial

As you can see there are some measures that will strengthen more than one asset for example:

M6, M11, M13 and M14 are linked and could benefit from regular blogging. M9 and M10 are linked and could both benefit by making the website work harder for the business.

M3 positioning and M4 brand recognition are linked and the proposed customer facing measures should help both.

Some affirmations will require more than one measure. If brand recognition is a problem you might choose an integrated marketing strategy combining a Mail Chimp campaign, LinkedIn Marketing, and pushing people to a new LinkedIn Group.

Weak Infrastructure assets will need to be strengthened as the business grows.

Brownbank's goal is to generate half a million pounds by the end of year 2. This Dream Ticket® is clearly indicating that the company is in its early stages of getting market recognition. If no-one knows the company exists it will be hard to get contracts and generate business. We typically recommend quarterly Dream Ticket® reviews but in the case of Brownbank we recommended a review after 45 days to make sure everything was working properly. If the indices of the market assets had not improved we would recommend reducing the revenue target and implementing some measures to control headcount so the business did not hire ahead of its revenue capability.

STEP 7: Cost the measures – Calculate the bill

Now it's time to look at the cost of investment to achieve the goal. Brownbank's measures are costed in Figure 12.7 below.

ASSET	INDEX	MEASURE	3 MONTH
MARKET			COST £k
M1	5	No action monitor	0
M2	5	No action monitor	0
M3	1+	For 30 days ask prospects what pops into their head when they hear our "name"	0
M4	1+	Ask 50 suspects if they recognise your brand	3
M5	1+	Approach customers for a satisfaction ranking then propose evangelism	0
M6	1	Blog weekly to the group	0
M7	1+	Approach customers asking for an endorsement	0
M8	1	Ask accounts to keep a historical customer log	0
M9	1	Measure for M10 should impact this	0
M10	1+	Ramp up on-line marketing. Make sure web site is on all documentation	4
M11	3+	Check weekly Analytics reports. Use Blogs in M6 on web site	1.5
M12	5	have the web site audited quarterly	0.5
M13	1	Measure for M6 should impact this	0
M14	1+	Measure for M6 should impact this	0
M15	1	Make four 2 minute videos	1.5
IP			
IP1	5	No action monitor	0
IP2	5	No action monitor	0
INFRASTR			
I1	5	No action monitor	0
I2	4+	No action monitor	0
I3	1+	Do an audit of IT systems ranking out of 5 for fit-for-purpose	0
I4	1+	Do an audit of business processes ranking out of 5 for fit-for-purpose	0
I5	5	No action monitor	0
I6	5	No action monitor	0
I7	1	Decide to trial Hootsuite	0
HUMAN			
H1	5	No action monitor	0
H2	5	No action monitor	0
H3	5	No action monitor	0
H4	5	No action monitor	0
		TOTAL	10.5

Figure 12.7 Brownbank Costing the Measures

Where possible I have recommended that Brownbank add some of the market research as part of their existing customer-facing activities. A spend of a few thousand pounds would give them some professional help for lead generation for a few weeks. Even though Brownbank is a small consulting company this Dream Ticket® would be similar for a larger consulting company, the projects and costs might be greater but the process identical. The Dream Ticket® methodology is scalable.

STEP 8: Review the plan and budget – Assign Actors, set a review period.

The next step is to plan to implement the measures. Who does what? What are the timelines for delivery? What is the review period?

During step 8 we assign actors to measures who will take on the task, and they need to have a review date. In Brownbank's Dream Ticket® I have recommended 45 days as these tasks are mostly done by people who are already in the company so the tasks are added to their work-load. If possible it's best to align review dates so the entire health of the Dream Ticket® can be assessed say quarterly. That said it would be a mistake to have long periods between reviewing critical assets that may move quickly.

	INDEX	MEASURE	ACTOR	REVIEW
MARKET				**DAYS**
M1	5	No action monitor		
M2	5	No action monitor		
M3	1+	For 30 days ask prospects what pops into their head when they hear our "name"	GERRY	45
M4	1+	Ask 50 suspects if they recognise your brand	ALISON	45
M5	1+	Approach customers for a satisfaction ranking then propose evangelism	GERRY	45
M6	1	Blog weekly to the group	JAMES	45
M7	1+	Approach customers asking for an endorsement	ALISON	45
M8	1	Ask accounts to keep a historical customer log	PAT	10
M9	1	Measure for M10 should impact this		
M10	1+	Ramp up on-line marketing. Make sure web site is on all documentation	ALISON	10
M11	3+	Check weekly Analytics reports. Use Blogs in M6 on web site	ALISON	45
M12	5	have the web site audited quarterly	ALISON	45
M13	1	Measure for M6 should impact this		
M14	1+	Measure for M6 should impact this		
M15	1	Make four 2 minute videos	ALISON	45
IP				
IP1	5	No action monitor		
IP2	5	No action monitor		
INFRASTR				
I1	5	No action monitor		
I2	4+	No action monitor		
I3	1+	Do an audit of IT systems ranking out of 5 for fit-for-purpose	PAT	45
I4	1+	Do an audit of business processes ranking ouit of 5 for fit-for-purpose	PAT	45
I5	5	No action monitor		
I6	5	No action monitor		
I7	1	Decide to trial Hootsuite	ALISON	45
HUMAN				
H1	5	No action monitor		
H2	5	No action monitor		
H3	5	No action monitor		
H4	5	No action monitor		

138

Figure 12.8 Brownbank Measures with Actors assigned

Now it's time look at figure 12.8, take a step back and with the team ask yourselves:

Does this plan hang together?

Can our team commit to and deliver the plan within the allotted time?

It may be the case that there are important measures in different categories, for example, beefing up customer databases and sales tracking systems in parallel with increasing repeat business. These tasks require different people skills, so more than one team. What is to be avoided is having so many measures that the efforts of team members are spread across too many tasks and so become diluted and ultimately ineffective.

Finally, take a look at the budget and ask yourself "With these tasks, and this team with this budget have we set ourselves up to achieve our goal?"

Remember what we are doing here is creating a situation so that in the future Brownbank will be able to achieve its goal. We are creating a healthy environment where sales will happen.

This is when the team may realise that the goal can't be met.

If the measures turned out to require a much larger investment it would be foolish to assume sales would still manifest. Then the budget needs to be increased to accommodate the measures OR the team should revise the goal, and go through the Dream Ticket® process again with a view to cutting the measures and re-costing them until there was a balance between the goal and the available budget.

STEP 9: Choose the ONE THING – what's the biggest bang for your buck?

If you are confronted with a large set of measures and not enough budget you could take the advice of Gary Keller and choose "THE ONE THING".

In his bestselling book Gary helps us to prioritise by way of a "focusing question".

> **"What's THE ONE THING I can do right now such that everything else will be easier or unnecessary?"**

Let me say that again.

> "What's THE ONE THING I can do right now such that everything else will be easier or unnecessary?"

Take a look at the measures in Brownbank's Dream Ticket® and ask yourself the focusing question "Which of all of the measures outlined could Brownbank do right now such that everything else will be easier or unnecessary."

I would say that M5 "We have 20 evangelists who will refer our services" is probably their ONE THING". I would choose this for a couple of reasons.

1. If each evangelist refers to 3 prospects that's 60 new clients
2. The evangelists can be the topic of the videos mentioned in M15. So initially a video with the first 3, then maybe 8 then 20. This would be a powerful marketing piece to put on the homepage of Brownbank's web site.

The key words in this question are "right now". Its desirable to get the entire company behind the ONE THING.

I have brought several products to market that require some form of standards compliance, medical devices, environmental devices and so forth and it takes years to gain compliance and a large budget. If complying with standards is mandatory and a year's work to achieve it's not going to make a difference in the short term. However, if it's the ONE THING that's mandatory you have to put plans in motion to achieve it and maybe find another way to generate revenue in the interim with a product or service that's faster to market with fewer legal constraints.

STEP 10: Plan and Review

We are now in a position to put all the measures, actors and dates into one plan and cut out those that you don't have the budget for putting the ONE THING at the top of the pile. The ONE THING is frequently a marketing action as many plans are revenue driven, meaning marketing actions are the assets that create the situation where sales can be made. Once drafted it's time to get the team to buy into the final plan and make sure everyone knows who is doing what. Take a step back to make sure that any interdependencies make sense with respect to time.

Keeping the process of delivering the measures on time requires regular review, at least every three months. A current favourite method is John Doerr's OKR (objectives, key results) system which is described in his excellent book "Measure What Matters". This method recommends focussing on a few objectives (measures), sharing and making them transparent throughout the company with employees able to see each other's progress against target. Even better, monthly reviews enable the team to see what's working and what's not, grading and colour coding progress as: no progress 0.0 to 0.3 (red), progress has been made but key results remain unmet 0.4 to 0.6 (yellow) and 0.7 to 1.0 (green) meaning key results are being met. This is a great way of getting the company to share the vision of the Dream Ticket and of course in turn builds great morale.

There are several software packages which you can use to implement OKRs.

What happens if there are several phases on the path to the Goal?

Consider a company called RAPIDSCAN that's developing a family of products that is able to identify bacterial contamination in liquid. They have a product roadmap that spans four years culminating in a product that's a medical device, so it needs to comply with regulatory standards.

RAPIDSCAN does not have the funds to carry the company for four years before launching its medical device, so on the journey to the medical device it plans to sell the same product to non-regulated markets, such as food and drink and veterinary. In this way, they have a phased marketing plan to develop credentials from early markets that they use to leverage themselves into new markets on the product roadmap.

Their plan for early revenues is to have four product launches let's call them P1, P2, P3, P4 where each product lays the foundations with endorsements and evangelists for the next product in the plan. So, in their Dream Ticket® we identified assets that will be activated in the future. You can see this in the table in Figure 12.9.

So, in their target in Figure 12.10, you can see seven market assets in pale blue whose start dates are phased in the future. This gives them the ability to both plan for the future and see the big picture.

	Asset	Active date	Index now	Measure	Actor	Review Date
M1	Memorable Names	Apr-18	1	Workshop	James	Aug-18
M2	Brand Recognition	Jun-20	1	Branding Work	Bella	Aug-20
M3	Positioning Company	Apr-18	1	Follow M2	Bella	Aug-18
M4	Positioning Product Line	Aug-18	1	Commence promotion	Bella	Jan-19
M5	Low Bounce	Apr-18	1	Web site Audit for SEO	Bella	Aug-18
M6	Web site	Dec-18	1	As above	Bella	Aug-19

M7	Endorsements P1	Apr-18	1	Identify 3 potentials	James	Dec-18
M8	Endorsements P2	Aug-19	1	As above	James	Jan-20
M9	Endorsements P3&P4	Oct-20	1	As above	James	Jan-21
M10	Evangelists P2	Mar-20	1	Research KOLS	James	Jun-20
M11	Evangelists P3&P4	Dec-21	1	Research KOLs	James	Mar-22
M12	Tribes	Apr-18	1	Find LinkedIn groups	James	Aug-18
M13	Brand Recognition	Apr-18	1	Blogs and Linked in	James	Aug-18

Figure 12.9 RAPIDSCAN Phased measures

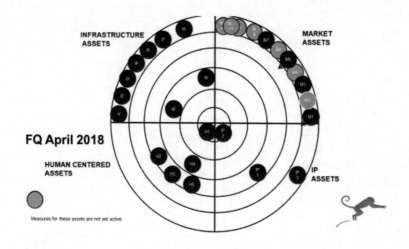

Figure 12.10 RAPIDSCAN Target with Phased Market Assets

Chapter 12 Summary

1. Plotting the assets on a target lets us see the status of the Dream Ticket® in a single view
2. Arrows on the dots indicate whether they are getting stronger, weaker or they are stuck.
3. New companies tend to have weak infrastructure assets and weak market assets.
4. Older companies need to regularly audit business processes to ensure they keep up to date with the company's needs
5. New companies need to have very strong human centred assets
6. For the assets that are below 5 choose measures that will strengthen them and propel them towards the centre of the target.
7. Some assets are linked therefore a single measure might strengthen more than one asset.
8. After costing the measures the budget might not be big enough, so reconsider what measures are essential and what's nice to have.
9. Assign actors to each measure and a completion date
10. Have interim short reviews before the completion date to catch problems early.
11. Where the budget won't support your chosen measures focus by choosing the ONE THING.
12. Where a company has a road-map over several years plan to activate measures over time.

Chapter 13

The Dream Ticket® Workshop

When I first started doing Intellectual Capital consulting we did audits, not workshops. My team used to do a huge amount of research to create the index. We used the methods described in chapters eight through eleven. If we wanted to test a Positioning statement we would do prospect interviews. We would look at every IT system in the company and determine who used them and why. We'd do brand recognition surveys and go through the company's invoices to see what percentage had bought again over a period of time. For a company with a few hundred people this was a massive amount of work and took weeks to complete.

Interestingly, on one occasion in Finland, when we were looking at invoices for repeat business our numbers did not match those presented in the accounts and we got thrown out as incompetent.

Fortunately, the key investor was a very good client of ours and this situation sparked his curiosity so he called in an auditor who discovered a couple of senior management were syphoning off cash from the company.

Luckily we were asked to go back! Oh joy!

In general after an audit when we presented our findings to the management team they pretty much agreed with them, commenting "Well no big surprises here". So I started to experiment by asking the management team to rank the assets before we did the research. The results of the executive team's "gut feel" was not very different from our findings after the research. Certainly, not different enough to warrant thousands of pounds of work and a project that was weeks long.

It was rare that one person would give an asset a 5 and his colleague a 1. Yes sometimes there was a disagreement over indexing but where we managed to remove territorial squabbles the team would mostly agree.

What they never got right was the list of assets they **should have** and how to prioritise their growth. They also did not realise that what they needed to do was create a set of future situations and scenarios that would mean they **could** achieve business goals.

Not one CEO has ever described to me a future business scenario they were aiming to create.

Sometimes CEOs have wanted to wait for a product launch, a reorganisation, or better sales results before doing a Dream Ticket® workshop.

This is backwards thinking.

Dream Ticket® workshops should come:

- Before writing the business plan
- Before reorganising the company
- Before you recruit new team members
- Before launching a new product
- And before re-planning a sales strategy

Dream Ticket® is a fabulous analytical process which prepares the company properly for all of the above in just 1 day!

A Dream Ticket® Workshop includes the workshop day, a report and a day with a 90-day review.

We kick off with a meeting of the management team to set the scenario for the exercise. Initially, I do a 40-minute presentation on the Dream Ticket® to demonstrate its power and set the stage for the rest of the day. I (or one of my colleagues) is the group moderator and our job is to challenge and push and poke the group where necessary so they think outside of the box.

Who should be on the Dream Ticket® Team®?

The Dream Ticket® workshop team typically comprises the management team and stakeholders in the goal. Who is in the room depends on what the goal is but it typically includes:

- The CEO, and CFO or divisional head
- Head of sales
- Head of marketing
- An operations person
- The CTO in a high tech company

This means there are probably about six to eight people in the room, anymore and it's hard to manage the group. The group moderator should not be from within the company as their role is to constantly challenge the decisions and observations of the group. The moderator needs to have quite a lot of experience in all aspects of the Dream Ticket® as we need to flip from marketing to IP to social media to distribution agreements to trademarks and so forth. It's quite a large skill set.

Each team member has a Dream Ticket® Workbook and the BIZVIZ® card deck. The BIZVIZ® card deck helps to solve the problem of the team not knowing what assets they should be growing. This is particularly true of market assets which have changed dramatically over recent years.

The workbook is currently on paper and can be downloaded from www.magicmonkey.eu/downloads.

The headings in the Workbook are:

- Asset ID (Identifier)
- Affirmation
- Current Index
- Measure
- Actor
- Review Period/date
- Budget

What are the pre-requisites for a Dream Ticket® Workshop?

There are a few things that must be in place before you can have a successful Dream Ticket® Workshop:

1. You must have a goal
2. You must know what your product or service is
3. You must have identified at least 1 market where the product will be targeted.
4. You must know the customer profile.

So let's get started

1. Agree on the Goal

The goal may come from an existing plan or indeed the team can create a goal of their own. There is also the issue of granularity to consider. The Dream Ticket® process works very well for SME's and divisions of larger companies. When dealing with a larger corporation there will need to be a hierarchy of Dream Tickets®. I have also worked with Dream Tickets® that only focus on one aspect of intangible assets such as Market. The key is to ensure that the team assigned to implement the measures is empowered to do so in order to get results. As no two companies are the same there is plenty of opportunity to get creative.

2. Choosing Assets with the BIZVIZ® Card Deck

The next step is to choose the assets that the company should have in order to achieve the goal. Some of these may be in place already, some the team "know" they should have but have not got around to putting in place yet. This is particularly true of market assets that relate to social media.

Figure 13.1

The BIZVIZ® card deck

The BIZVIZ® card deck comprises four cards that explain each of the asset categories: market, intellectual property, human-centred and infrastructure and forty-seven cards each describing the asset (as in Chapters two through five in this book). Each asset card has three push questions for the team to consider.

Each team member has a card deck and together with the team chooses the cards and assets that need to be on their Dream Ticket®. At the end of the exercise, each team member has the same 2 piles of cards those to be on the Dream Ticket® and those to be left out. If the team is familiar with the content of the card deck this process typically takes around 30 minutes. Where team members are not familiar with the nature of intangible assets the process takes a bit longer.

Design the Affirmations

The affirmations are chosen and agreed by the team and each entered into the workbook. As it's likely that each Dream Ticket® will have 25 to 35 affirmations this can take a couple of hours. Key is to pick an affirmation that can be measured in some way and is as focussed as possible. The affirmation is entered into the workbook next to the asset.

3. Index Assets (Look back to today)

Indexing the assets is the next step. A value between one (weak) and five (strong) is assigned to each asset. This task typically fleshes out some disagreement between team members, especially if a team member has responsibility for an asset that gets a weak index. It's the job of the moderator to assist the team in having an ego-free debate on the index. It's rare there will be disagreement with one person assigning a 1 and another assigning a 5 for the same asset, more likely a debate over a 2 or 3. A prolonged debate is an indication that this particular asset requires proper research using the methods outlined in Chapters 8 through 11.

That said, regular customer interviews for feedback on the company and its performance and regular interviews for Positioning and brand recognition should be a permanent resident on every Dream Ticket®.

In my workshops I like to use lots of colour so I give a colour to each asset class for example market assets are pink, human-centred assets are blue, IP assets are green and Infrastructure assets are orange.

4. Plotting your Dream Ticket®

Plotting the Dream Ticket® is the next step. In the workbook, I have the targets already printed with the associated colours for each asset category. Armed with sticky coloured dots the team writes the asset number M1, M2, M3 onto their pink dots, H1, H2, H3 onto blue dots and so forth then sticks them into the appropriate quadrant on the target, as you can see in Figure 13.2.

The Target

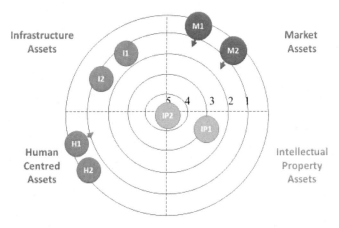

Infrastructure Assets

Market Assets

Human Centred Assets

Intellectual Property Assets

Figure 13.2 Colour Coded Target

More information is conveyed by the coloured dots as by the time the team has finished the target will typically be dominated by one colour – so a "pink" company or a green company and so forth. Software is under development to automate this process however the kindergarten element of this exercise is typically appreciated by the management team!

5. Choosing the measures that will close the gap

Choosing the measures that will close the gap is the most time-consuming part of the Dream Ticket® Workshop as there may be several different ways to close the gap. Also look at the relationship between assets as some measures will have an impact on more than one asset.

Money is almost always an issue so using systems that are already in place to gather information for the Dream Ticket® process is a great idea.

Ask accounts to have a monthly league table of repeat customers by value.

When contacting a new suspect or prospect, ask them if they have ever heard of your company or product name before. If they have, then follow up with "Oh good, what's the first thing that pops into your head when you think about this company". This will validate your positioning statement or tell you when you have a problem.

Ask existing customers how frequently they have heard from a local distributor. Rarely will one campaign on a single asset have the desired impact, you have to keep plugging away with campaigns two or three times before you begin to see changes.

6. Cost the measures

Costing the measures may take a few days to do properly, however, in the Dream Ticket® Workshop, you can get a sense of budget size. You want to complete all of the 10 steps of the workshop in one day.

Firstly, go through the measures and see which ones can be tackled as part of existing processes. These are effectively freebees as long as they are not too time-consuming. Take care the sales team doesn't get bogged down with marketing instead of sales, or administration gets lost in data collection. Unless you have huge numbers of customers you won't have to do large exercises to get a sense of what the customer/distributor or evangelist thinks about your company.

7. Review the budget, Assign Actors

Having costed and sized the measures it's time to take a view on which measures to back and which have to be put on hold. Look at how the existing budget is allocated. Does it make any sense? Are you spending resources pushing sales where you have no case studies, endorsements or evangelists? Are you planning to enter territories without local credentials? American customers will want endorsements from other American customers not customers in France.

Re-purpose existing budgets to strengthen assets so you hit goals and get those dots into the centre of the target. Assign measures to individuals and set deadlines.

8. The Focusing Question THE ONE THING!

Get group consensus on THE ONE THING.

By now the team will have been together for almost a day so it's time to drive towards closure. The team should be feeling pretty good about themselves, the company and the plan. Seeing the future and success is so much more fun than wondering what to do, so team morale should be high.

9. Plan and Review

Plan how you are going to monitor and review. Initially have short meetings regularly to make sure measures are on track – weekly for just 30 minutes is a good idea to keep up momentum. Make the Dream Team dial-in or Skype for meetings so they are not a great distraction from other aspects of the business. Make sure the team remains a team even though they may not have any actions, don't let 1 or 2 people become a subset to deliver the measures.

At the end of the workshop, I always ask the team how they feel about the Dream Ticket®. Most always, the response I get is that change is required to hit the goal and be successful.

I emphasise again, before starting to write a business plan the team run a Dream Ticket® Workshop. Thinking about it it's obvious. Using Business Visualisation and The Dream Ticket® Methodology sets out the direction to get from today to the goal. Yes, like snakes and ladders there will be pitfalls but that just means rethinking priorities and measures.

The Dream Ticket® Workbook®

Figures 13.2 to 13.5 show an example of what parts of the Dream Ticket® Workbook will look like when complete. As you can see there are a number of assets that have zero cost assigned as an existing staff member will take this task on.

Figure 13.2 Market Assets

1	2	3	4	5	6	7	8	9	10
ID	Asset	Affirmation	DT goal	Current status	Measure	Current Index	Actor	Review period	Budget
M1	Brand recognition	80% of prospects recognise our brand	80%	<10%	Mail chimp promotion	1+	Hayley	45 days	zero
M2	Low bounce rate	>2 minute visit	50%	<30 seconds	Add video content Add free offers	1	Hayley	45 days	£5,000
M3									
M4									

Figure 13.3 Human Centred Assets

ID	Asset	Affirmation	DT Goal	Current Status	Measure	Current Index	Actor	Review period	Budget
H1	Passion	All employees are passionate about product quality	100%		Print name of employee who assembled on product packaging	1+	James	45 days	Zero external cost
H2	Work related competencies	All employees know how to assemble our product	100%		Introduce product assembly into initiation process	1	James	45 days	Zero external cost
H3									
H4									

Figure 13.4 Intellectual Property Assets

ID	Asset	Affirmation	DT index	Current Status	Measure	Current index	Actor	Review Period	Budget
IP1	Patents	All products are protected by 3 patents	100	Most protected by 2	Get patent education for engineers from our IP lawyers	3	Annie	45 days	Zero external cost
IP2	Trademarks	All brands are trademarked	100		none	5	Annie		£4,000
IP3									
IP 4									

Figure 13.5 Infrastructure Assets

ID	Asset	Affirmation	DT index	Current Status	Measure	Current index	Actor	Review Period	Budget
I1	Standards	We have FDA approval for X	100%	In process 1 years to go	Complete approval in 12 months	3+	Toby	monthly	£150K
I2	Standards	All Databases are GDPR compliant	50%	Process underway	Complete opt – in scheme	3+	Toby	Monthly	Zero externa l cost
I3									
I4									

At the End of the Day

Planning a business is typically the remit of the CEO and a couple of others on the management team. That means that plans get handed down to others that may not have had any input to the process. The Dream Ticket® Workshop is a fabulous team building exercise that looks at the business holistically. It's an opportunity to soften barriers that might exist between different departments. At the end of the Dream Ticket® Workshop, if everyone is not revved up something is very wrong!

Chapter 13 Summary

1. Get the team to estimate the index for each asset
2. Where there is any debate always mount a formal measure to choose the index
3. Management teams typically don't have a vision of how the company will look years hence

4. Dream Ticket® workshops should come:
    - Before writing the business plan
    - Before reorganising the company
    - Before you recruit new team members
    - Before launching a new product
    - And before re-planning a sales strategy
5. A Dream Ticket® Workshop takes just 1 day
6. Choose the members of the Dream Ticket® team to reflect the goal
7. The Dream Ticket® Moderator should not be from the company

8. The Dream Ticket® Workbook can be downloaded from www.magicmonkey.eu
9. Use the BIZVIZ® card deck to understand and choose the assets
10. Plot the Dream Ticket® Target in the workshop using the coloured dots
11. Assign measures to existing staff where feasible
12. Initially have regular short reviews of measures
13. Team morale at the end of The Dream Ticket® Workshop should be very high

Chapter 15

Back to Planning and Goals

So let's go back to writing plans and choosing goals

Here you are, the CEO or perhaps a management team or Divisional Director, required to write a business plan and set business goals for the next three years. It might be to raise funds, to provide a benchmark to compare company performance or just as a roadmap for the business.

Business Plans are typically not "live" documents and don't take into consideration change until it's time for them to be replaced for a new business period.

No matter what the reason, the plan will probably have a familiar contents page with most of these headings.

1. Relevant company data, contacts, contact data, logos etc.
2. Executive Summary
3. Background
    a. History
    b. Business Objectives
4. Industry Overview
5. Product or Service Description
6. Target Market Segment

7. Business Opportunity
8. Competition
9. R&D
10. Standards and Regulations
11. Quality and Assurance
12. Manufacturing
13. Marketing Strategy
14. Customer Profile
15. Distribution Strategy
16. Risk Analysis
17. Personnel
18. Ownership (Capital Structure)
19. Exit strategy (for companies seeking to raise finance)
20. Sales Forecasts
21. Financial data
    a. Budget
    b. Financial Projections

In fact, my template which I use to create business plans, is much bigger having around 60 possible titles just for the MRD (Market Requirements Document).

Taking a look at some of these titles the contents of these sections is temporal, meaning they change over time and sometimes require predicting what the business will be doing in the future. In particular:

1. **The Product or Service Description** – if it's a new product you might not know what features it will require in 3 years' time. Even so with existing products, there may be new requirements as the market changes

2. **The Business Opportunity** – this section requires predicting future market conditions.
3. **The Business Objectives** – these can't be nailed down until you understand the future environment the business is required to operate in.
4. **The Market** – this is a moving target as the market and its requirements evolve and competitors come and go and also change.
5. **Standards and regulations** – these are constantly changing and being amended
6. **Marketing Strategy** – this has to be appropriate for the climate the business is operating in at can at best be a guess about the future.
7. **Risk Analysis** – this takes into consideration technical, market and competitive risk but its assessing future risk, time being the most unpredictable for new products and services.
8. **Personnel** – what is the nature of the future employee? What skills will the company require over the years to come?
9. **Sales Forecasts** – on what basis is the sales forecast made? A percentage of a potential market or the bandwidth of the distribution channel? In either case, it's very unpredictable unless it's a business that selling repeat products to a market that's required to purchase.
10. **Budget** – the required funds to achieve the business objectives. This is at best a guess as the activities of the company will change in response to the business climate.

So you can see that there is too much guesswork in this approach as none of the business planning techniques we currently use actually aim to predict what the environment is going to be like for YOUR product in the future.

Or maybe you have your plan and are striving to hit it. You are a business leader and things are not going as well as predicted. Sales are a bit low, you have a few HR problems or you are about to launch a new product and wondering what you might have forgotten.

In what way will Dream Ticket® help you?

Think about our mountain again.

If you had to make a plan to climb a mountain where would you rather be? At the top of the mountain having experienced the climb, or at the bottom struggling to see the summit through the clouds?

Whilst Dream Ticket® is certainly no crystal ball, it gives us insight into how we can envisage the future and with regular review keep modifying the strategy and tactics to stay on course for the climb. Where the business plan is mostly about WHAT the business will do, with not too much on HOW, the Dream Ticket® tells us much more.

1. Where our strengths and weaknesses are
2. What we need to do to make the company stronger
3. How long this process will take

4. How we can create a favourable future business climate to sell our products and services
5. Whether our messaging to the market is on track to make prospects buy
6. If our branding is working
7. Whether we are encouraging repeat business
8. If our prospects and customers think positively about the business
9. Whether our digital marketing strategy is fit for purpose
10. If our website is an asset or a liability
11. Whether the distribution channel is working to generate business
12. If we are creating and using endorsements and evangelists
13. How we are measuring up against plan over time
14. How we are positioned in the market against our competitors
15. Who is responsible for all of the measures to make the business stronger
16. Completion dates for assigned measures
17. If our IP portfolio delivers good ROI and adds value to the business
18. If we are managing shareholders and investors appropriately
19. If our corporate culture and management philosophy are working to help or hinder the business
20. Whether we have the right people in the business to achieve its goals
21. How to identify and protect critical knowledge functions
22. If the infrastructure is appropriate to protect and support the business and its processes.

23. If we have the right advisors for the company
24. If there is enough money in the budget to achieve the goal
25. Whether we need to modify our plan or our goal. In this way, we are able to predict whether we can be successful or whether we need to re-plan.

With your hand on your heart can you say "yes" you have all of this information about your business right now? I thought not.

Yet, if you do have to write a business plan, let's consider what Dream Ticket® Workshop will arm you with.

The ten steps in Dream Ticket® give you 10 things you will need to plan:

1. The goal sets the mission

2. The assets are the shopping list for success

3. The affirmations set the strategy to achieve the goal

4. The indices give a clear view of the current status of the company relative to its goal

5. The target shows the strengths and weaknesses of the company in a single view

6. The measures are the tactical plan

7. Costing the measures provides the basis for the budget

8. The review tells the company if it can achieve the goal with current resources or one or both needs to be changed

9. The ONE THING provides focus

10. The three-month review is an early warning system if the goal can't be met and provides us with the opportunity to change and refine the affirmations and measures.

Business plans and Dream Tickets® are synergistic. The Dream Ticket® is the process which, **if kept live** will ensure we hit the business plan goals AND give us an early warning system if we are about to lose our way giving us the opportunity to re-plan.

Dream Ticket® is a holistic method. The business plan sets the goal and objectives and that's fine, but the Dream Ticket® delivers the battle plan that has to be dynamic and serve the needs of the business over time.

Dream Ticket® is the most comprehensive business analysis and planning method on the market today, that's superb for our digital age because of the huge number of intangible assets businesses now have.

This is why the Dream Ticket® is so powerful and should be completed before committing to a business plan.

Remember the only four things you need to know before commencing are:

1. The goal

2. The target market

3. A product or service definition with its features and benefits

4. The customer profile

The Dream Ticket® Workshop takes just 1 day.

So, what are you waiting for? Let's do it!

About The Author

Annie Brooking is a serial entrepreneur and CEO and has brought nineteen high technology products to market in Silicon Valley, Boston, Iceland and the UK.

She is the author of three business books "Intellectual Capital", Corporate Memory and Dream Ticket®. She is currently working on her fourth book which is about product marketing.

Annie has her own consulting company Magic Monkey, runs Dream Ticket® Workshops and helps companies that are bringing new products to market based on disruptive technologies.

In her early career she taught computer science at various Universities and colleges in the UK.

Annie lives in Cambridge, UK with her husband Leighton and can be contacted at annie@magicmonkey.eu